THE ROYAL ENGINEERS IN KOREA
THE PHOTOGRAPHIC MEMOIR OF FRANK MERRITT

MATT MERRITT

Pen & Sword
MILITARY

AN IMPRINT OF PEN & SWORD BOOKS LTD.
YORKSHIRE - PHILADELPHIA

First published in Great Britain in 2024 by
PEN AND SWORD MILITARY
An imprint of
Pen & Sword Books Ltd
Yorkshire – Philadelphia

Copyright © Matt Merritt, 2024

ISBN 978 1 39904 469 1

The right of Matt Merritt to be identified as Author of this work has been asserted by him in accordance with the Copyright, Designs and Patents Act 1988.

A CIP catalogue record for this book is available from the British Library

All rights reserved. No part of this book may be reproduced or transmitted in any form or by any means, electronic or mechanical including photocopying, recording or by any information storage and retrieval system, without permission from the Publisher in writing.

Typeset in Times New Roman 11/13 by SJmagic DESIGN SERVICES, India.
Printed and bound in the UK by CPI Group (UK) Ltd.

Pen & Sword Books Ltd incorporates the imprints of Pen & Sword Archaeology, Atlas, Aviation, Battleground, Discovery, Family History, History, Maritime, Military, Naval, Politics, Social History, Transport, True Crime, Claymore Press, Frontline Books, Praetorian Press, Seaforth Publishing and White Owl

For a complete list of Pen & Sword titles please contact

PEN & SWORD BOOKS LIMITED
George House, Units 12 & 13, Beevor Street, Off Pontefract Road,
Barnsley, South Yorkshire, S71 1HN, England
E-mail: enquiries@pen-and-sword.co.uk
Website: www.pen-and-sword.co.uk

or

PEN AND SWORD BOOKS
1950 Lawrence Rd, Havertown, PA 19083, USA
E-mail: uspen-and-sword@casematepublishers.com
Website: www.penandswordbooks.com

Contents

Introduction vi

Chapter 1	From England to Japan 1
Chapter 2	Capchong and Kamak-san 13
Chapter 3	The Korean People 26
Chapter 4	The River 42
Chapter 5	Korean Service Corps 50
Chapter 6	'Scheme 1' 55
Chapter 7	'Scheme 2' 65
Chapter 8	'Scheme 3' 77
Chapter 9	Stalemate 92
Chapter 10	Tockchong 96
Chapter 11	Seoul 102
Chapter 12	Tokyo 115
Chapter 13	Winter 140
Chapter 14	The Road 144
Chapter 15	The Castle Inn 156
Chapter 16	Homeward Bound 179

Acknowledgements 202
Bibliography and Sources 203

Introduction

In the Korean War section of the Royal Engineers Museum is a copy of their in-house magazine *The Kansas Tract, Journal of the Royal Imjineers* (a pun on the name of the River Imjin and engineers). On the page displayed is an image of 'Sapper Newson Piloting a Power Boat on The River Imjin'. My father, Frank Merritt, took this photograph. He was both a sapper and a war photographer, but his large archive has remained unseen until now.

Frank's Box Brownie Six-20 Model D camera was made in Britain in 1953. The quality of the workmanship means the camera and its canvas case are still in good condition today. The camera is made of heavy-duty sheet metal wrapped in imitation black leather with a horizontal line design on the faceplate. It has a Meniscus F/11 100mm portrait lens. It has two ice-cube-like glass image finders: one next to the leather strap handle provides a top-down view and the other is on the side. To take a picture, the camera has a side-mounted plastic push button that operates a single-blade shutter. There is a plastic winding wheel to roll on the 3 inch by 2.5 inch film roll. The film is loaded into the back of the camera by opening its hinged back. The back locks into place by a triangular spring catch on the top of the camera body. On the side, where the shutter and the winding wheel are positioned, are metal contacts for a flashgun.

In his army camp in Korea, Frank acquired the chemicals he needed to develop his films. He made the envelopes of his negative albums out of folded-over sheets of paper and stapled them together into books with cream paper covers. Frank also took two 35mm cameras to Korea. For the film negative albums, he used blank folded-over notepaper to make envelopes with blue paper covers. The 35mm films were cut into strips of two, three or four photographs in length. Some were fire damaged around the edges, possibly because a stove had overheated, setting Frank's tent ablaze. However, the actual photographs survived intact.

Imagine assembling several complex jigsaw puzzles simultaneously. However, the pieces are mixed together in one heap and there are no pictures to use as a guide. That was the challenge I faced in writing this book, with only remembered conversations with my father to work from.

Introduction vii

Discovered in the bottom of Frank's wardrobe was his Box Brownie camera and handmade negative albums for his Korean archive, created more than seventy years ago.

Although it was never formally diagnosed, Frank was on the autistic spectrum. He was also dyslexic, and it was rare for him to write anything down. When he was called up for National Service in the 1950s during the Korean War, he could have deferred being as he was a farmer's son and farming a reserved occupation. Feeling, however, it was his duty to serve, he joined the Royal

Engineers. When my father arrived on the frontline in Korea, Captain Sharp of 3 Troop, 55 Independent Field Squadron, 28th Field Engineer Regiment didn't know what to do with him as he was unconventional and rebellious. Then, the captain discovered Frank's keen interest in photography, and he became the unit's photographer.

My father took it upon himself to explore Korea, believing wholeheartedly in the 'join the army and see the world' motto the recruiting sergeant had given him. He often wandered off alone, through an active war zone, blithely unconcerned, with nothing but his camera. The Korean people were surprised to see a United Nations soldier strolling through their villages and farms unarmed and taking photographs. Frank went into places that were off limits due to enemy activity and was able to take the kind of candid photographs of ordinary Korean people going about their daily lives, scenes that are not to my knowledge available from any other source.

In Korea Frank built his own photographic enlarger to print his pictures.

I found while researching this book that Frank's dyslexia meant the lettering and numbering of his photograph albums was sometimes duplicated and often appeared to be in reverse order. He would write brief, misspelled notes on the album covers that gave little indication of what the photographs were of, where they were taken and when. Some of the square negatives of Brownie film or the negative strips of 35mm film within these albums didn't match up with the notes on the covers. His service record too gave me more questions than answers. Fortunately, the Korean War Diaries at the Royal Engineers Museum were able to provide some of the details.

Some of the negative strips had been unevenly cut and, with careful examination, a film roll could be pieced back together to run consecutively by frame number. Frustratingly, not all the film brands used had frame numbers to work by. Often, the middle strips that may have linked the start and end of a film were lost. Several filmstrips had the same frame numbers, which led me to realize that Frank had two 35mm cameras. He had mentioned using a Leotax camera and in one photograph was pictured with a brown leather case, possibly for an Agfa Sillette camera.

Frank rather randomly glued his prints into his treasured, black-paged albums. Several negatives are missing for prints that exist in these albums, and I suspect a third album may have been lost. Frank also built a wooden box to keep his colour slides in. However, the pictures of a stopover in Cyprus on his way to or back from Korea were missing, leaving empty slide frames and badly scratched pictures that were scanned and stored on a CD.

Today, Frank's cameras are like time machines. His photographic archive provides a unique and valuable insight into the life of the Korean people and the British military during the Korean War. I hope his photographs ensure that both the civilians and Frank's comrades who were caught up in this conflict are not forgotten.

Chapter 1

From England to Japan

Frank was born on 30 August 1932. His family lived in village cottages near rented land at Chalk in Kent, which his father farmed as a market garden. At 7 years old, Frank played with a toy Meccano kit, building motorized models of cranes and bridges in his bedroom. Frank's first camera was an eighth birthday present in 1940. From then on, he never went anywhere without a camera, wanting to photo document everything he saw.

Growing up during the Second World War, Frank knew little about the world outside his home. The family didn't read newspapers, there was no TV and they rarely listened to radio. Frank knew when he stood in the fields of the family's farm that the planes flying overhead were German bombers on their way to destroy towns and cities.

Frank aged 14.

The tractor's cankerous engine troubled Frank's father until a German prisoner of war came to work on the farm. The German didn't need to be guarded as he had wanted no part in the mass murder of those who couldn't defend themselves. He also had no time for schoolboys curious about engineering as he serviced the tractor engine in the barn. Frank quickly learned the German word for 'out'.

The German was a welcomed guest at the kitchen table for a meal as Frank's parents saw him as somebody else's son far from home. Frank's father hoped the kindness would be repaid if Frank or his brother Ted were ever in a similar situation.

At the end of the war in 1945, the German was repatriated. Germany had been split into zones of occupation by the allies. In the west, the British, French and

Frank's father, Albert, owned a 1938 Fordson tractor. It had ridged metal rims covering the wheels as rubber tyres didn't exist for farm machinery.

Americans had subdivided the nation into zones of control. They also controlled the city of Berlin in the Soviet zone of what became East Germany. Frank never discovered what happened to the German he had come to regard as a friend.

In June 1945, Frank was 12 years old when his mother died. Frank had to take over the running of the house and look after his younger brother. His father, then aged 55, continued to work the farm. Frank's father suffered from partial paralysis in his arm as he had been shot on the Western Front in the First World War (1914–18). The bullet had punched through the pay book in his top-right tunic pocket and entered his arm, badly damaging the muscle. In the First World War all soldiers had to carry a pay book in their top-right pocket as identification. An unknown surgeon had saved his life and the arm.

Frank's father's generation never talked about the First World War, but for many of them, recalling the horror at night was inescapable. Albert awoke at the slightest noise. Guy Fawkes Night was the family's most hated night of the year. The fireworks reminded Albert of being head down in the mud of a trench as the world above him exploded. Waking his father from his nightmares to go to work, Frank had to keep a safe distance. After his own service in Korea, Frank had the same issues on awakening.

After a long working day, Frank's father sat in his armchair by the fire reading Shakespeare or Dickens. Despite his dyslexia, Frank studied books on engineering and architecture, and analysed technical drawings to learn how things were put together and how they worked. The school leaving age was 14 and Frank proudly left in 1946 with his certificate for 'chair making'. His school had seemed designed for national conformity, a factory churning out standard workers for Britain to employ in its industries. Frank went to work on the farm.

On 19 December 1946, fighting broke out between the Soviet-backed communist Viet-Minh and French colonial forces in Indochina (now known as Laos, Cambodia and Vietnam). On 24 June 1948, in response to the British, French and American plan to create West Germany, the Soviet Union cut off the Allied-controlled city of Berlin in East Germany. A city of two million was left without food and power. If the Western allies attempted to break the blockade by shipping supplies through the Soviet zone, it would have started a third world war. It seemed inevitable that atomic bombs would be used to wipe out one city after another, starting with the complete destruction of Berlin. The solution for the Western allies was the Berlin Airlift codenamed Operation Vittles. A constant stream of freight aircraft delivered more than two million tons of cargo. Sixty-seven per cent was coal for Berlin's power stations and twenty-four per cent was food, with the remaining per cent listed as sundries. More than 85,000 tons of Berlin-manufactured goods were exported by air from the city to keep its economy going. The operation was a success, with the Soviet siege ending on 30 September 1949.

On the other side of the world, Japan had occupied Korea since 1910. The Second World War had ended this situation in 1945. Korea was politically divided with the north being run by the Soviet Union, while the USA and its allies had liberated the south. On 15 August 1948, South Korea was recognized by the United Nations as a new country – the Republic of Korea. The communist north became the Democratic People's Republic of Korea on 9 September 1948, as recognized in October by the Soviet Union.

Following a series of infiltration attacks upon the border, at 4am on 25 June 1950, North Korea invaded South Korea. The North Korean People's Army (NKPA) outnumbered the Republic of Korea Army (ROKA) and American forces, who had only a week's supply of ammunition between them. The United Nations Assembly comprised member states whose aim was to avert a third world war involving the use of atomic weapons. When they voted for a resolution calling for North Korea to withdraw, it was ignored and so the United Nations mobilized for war.

By 1952, the war had been raging for two years when Frank's National Service call-up papers dropped through the letterbox. He was then aged 20. His father placed them on the kitchen table in front of him at breakfast. Frank was now caught between the worlds of politics, civilian and military life. Frank's father thought those worlds were changing too fast and leaving the poor and the vulnerable behind. He led a quiet, private life, where he was the head of his household, and where his sons were concerned, his word was final.

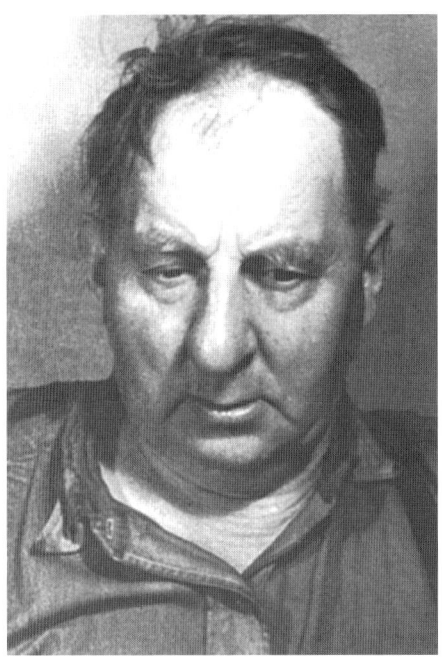

Frank's father.

Frank's father's younger brother, Percy, had been a regular soldier and was killed in action in 1914. It had been during his first week of setting his boots on French soil in the First World War. He had died at 20 years of age and been buried in France. Percy's medal had been sent to his brother, who after the war also received the 'Dead Man's Penny'. This was a plaque of 4.5 inches in diameter cast in bronze. The face depicted a lion standing beside Lady Britannia laying a laurel wreath upon a box bearing Percy's raised engraved name. This casting used a lost technique to emboss the names, making each of the approximately one million plaques a treasured keepsake for the next of kin. Frank's father, like many others, could not afford to visit his brother's grave in France. With the plaque came a scroll bearing the Royal Crest and the king's condolence message with Percy's name handwritten in calligraphic script. Albert's brother-in-law was killed on 21 March 1918 during the last German offensive of the First World War. Albert's sister also received a 'Dead Man's Penny'.

On 4 September 1952, Frank reported to begin his two years' National Service and joined 3 Training Regiment Royal Engineers at Cove in Hampshire. He told me that every recruit quickly became lost in the barracks with impatient, non-commissioned officers bawling them out to set the standard of discipline. Everyone needed to learn and experience what a sergeant's wrath was like, so they would obey orders. The sergeant's wrath was legendary and even the officers were intimidated. The corporals rounded up the new recruits to parade before the sergeant in symmetrical rows. They stood to attention, looking up at the sky and not daring to make eye contact with the sergeant. His swagger stick was tucked into his armpit. It looked as if he had been impaled with it, as he stood chest out, shoulders back and his peaked cap so low his piercing eyes stared out from beneath the brim. He bellowed in a guttural voice insulting parents and saying, as Frank recalled, 'You don't know you're born!'

Frank thought, 'What have I got myself into?' He was hoping the sergeant would walk down the line and pick on someone else as he was told how army life was going to be. The sergeant could read your mind and see into your very soul

When Frank left Chalk village all he wanted, like his father before him, was to retain the chivalry and personal honour that the family lived by.

as he looked each man up and down. Frank said, 'The one thing he didn't do was be vulgar and call you this, that or the other because profanity was beneath him.'

The sergeant had told the men, 'My time is precious, and I have to turn you – a misfit rabble from… .' He rattled off the names of random towns, 'into what?' He had glared expectantly. 'Soldiers!' the parade had chorused in unison at the top of their lungs.

Basic training involved:

- How to pack the clothes you arrived in with regimented precision into a brown paper parcel tied up with string. With a ruler, the sergeant measured the knotted bows to ensure they were the length the army insisted upon. This parade of parcels was home addressed, postage stamped and put into sacks to, in the sergeant words, 'aggravate the collecting postman's bad back'.
- How to wash – scrubbing your body from head to foot in the shower with the bar of caustic soap you were given. The sergeant advised, 'using a circular motion to create plenty of lather like window cleaning'.

- How to shave so your face was smooth with no 'bluff fluff' as the sergeant called stubble.
- How to 'spit and polish' black boots so they were mirrors on the inspection parade. The sergeant shouted at Frank, 'That's no good – you can't see your face in them to shave!'
- How to dress – uniforms pressed and ironed, belt buckles and buttons polished and gleaming for the inspection parade.
- How to make your bed. The itchy blankets had to be tucked in at all four 'hospital' corners, as they were called. The pillow felt like a brick.
- How to set out your kit on your bed. This was your clothing, boots, mess tins and metal cup, etc., for inspection. Frank recalled, 'The slightest speck of dirt and it all ended up on the barrack room floor, mattress and all.'
- How to march. The recruits found themselves square bashing the parade ground, with arms swinging, legs striding out, and the sergeant bellowing 'Left! Right! Left! Right! About turn!'
- Then there were the training runs to build up fitness and endless push-ups. Limbs became tough as tree trunks and the sergeant said, 'You're showing the muscles you never knew you had.'

Nobody had yet earned the right to call the sergeant 'Sarge' and the only words he wanted to hear were 'Yes sergeant!' In a moment of sudden rebellious anger, Frank expressed the fact he wanted to kill him, and the sergeant beamed with delight and said, 'My job is done.' Frank was puzzled by this reaction. The sergeant had given him what he needed to stay alive. He had awakened a prehistoric survival instinct in Frank, but it didn't mean Frank was ready to kill anyone.

The sergeant had made Frank more confident in himself. As a child, he'd had a stammer, but now he didn't stutter in conversation anymore. The sergeant had told him to 'think of words other than the ones you're struggling to say'. For the first time, Frank was able to speak coherently in his rasping chainsaw voice. This was something he had not previously achieved and been bullied for at school. When he'd arrived in barracks, he had been the complete opposite of the city urchins full of false bravado that they usually received. Instead, he'd been a shy, suit-and-tie-wearing farm boy, more used to heaving around sacks of his father's potatoes than dealing with people.

Frank got through the six weeks of basic training. He then trained for the Standard Tactical Trial and on 6 February 1953 passed to qualify as a B3 field engineer. According to his service record, on 2 March 1953, Frank was 'Struck of Strength' as it was termed on the 3 Training Regiment list. The medical assessment stamps marked his service record as 'FE' for 'Fitness Excellent'. Frank was a smart, athletic soldier when he left the training barracks for his regimental posting. He joined A Squadron Independent Field Royal Engineers at the Royal Engineer depot at Barton Stacey, Hampshire, on 3 March.

On 8 April 1953, his Home Service ended after a total of 217 days. On the next day, he was 'Struck of Strength' and his record stated 'ERE [Extra Regimental Employment] proceeding with Draft DCDUQ Korea posted to Korean Theatre.'

Among Frank's photographic archive was a blank souvenir postcard he purchased of Her Majesty's Troopship *Empire Pride* (ship number 168687). She had been built in the Clydeholm Yard, Glasgow, by Barclay, Curle & Co. Ltd. The ship was owned by the Ministry of War Transport and was operated by Bibby Bros. & Co. Glasgow. The *Empire Pride* had been in continuous service since her launch in the Second World War in 1941. On its military deployment, troops would run the length of its 494.2-feet deck to maintain their fitness. HMT *Empire Pride* was 64.4-feet wide, and her gross cargo tonnage was initially listed as 8418 tons. When the ship left Liverpool for Korea, she was carrying 9248 tons as reported by newspapers including the *Portsmouth Evening News* of Friday, 10 April 1953.

On the troop decks of the *Empire Pride* were 1444 hammocks for the enlisted men to sleep in. Conditions were considered 'generally satisfactory' as had been earlier claimed in a statement made in the House of Commons Troopship (Amenities) Debate on 13 November 1951. This was not, however, my father's experience. On his first sea voyage, Frank hated bedding down in the swinging net hammock strung up in a cramped, stuffy and hot berth containing hundreds of men. The banter was raucous and constant. There was the squeal of cutlery scraping mass-produced, barely edible food from mess tins, and the scrunch of men tackling slices of bread that were as hard as paving slabs. The stamp of running soldiers' boots upon the deck plating above accompanied the slam of access hatches and the thunderous mechanical heartbeat of the ship's two M4 cylinder, 9000hp two-screw engines. There were also the random bangs and crashes due to changes in

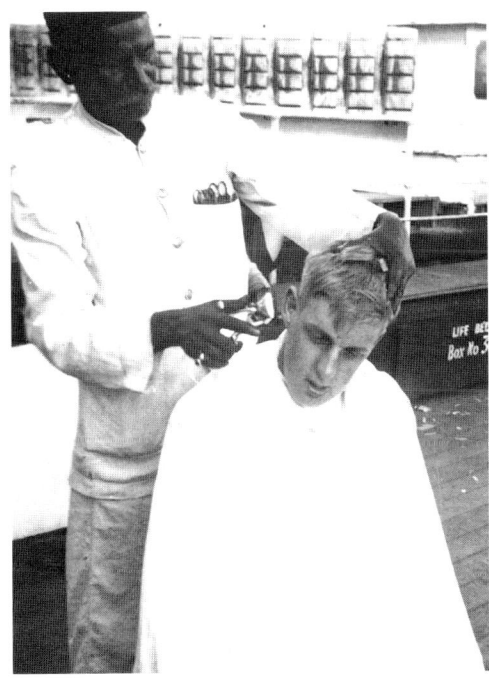

The intense training for combat meant Frank had little time to photograph life on board the troopship. Frank was photographed getting a haircut on an open deck of the HMT Empire Pride. The army cut was a number four comb guard on the clippers for the top of the head and a number two for the back and sides. For Frank, it was a chance to escape from the overcrowded hold.

Troopships for Korea docked at Kure, Japan – a port on the inland sea near the city of Hiroshima in the province of Honshu.

atmospheric pressure and sea temperature. It was these sounds that gave the HMT *Empire Pride* its personality. To Frank, she felt alive.

Frank walked the open deck when the *Empire Pride* sailed through the warmer waters of the Mediterranean and later the Arabian Sea. The sight of flying fish and dolphins leaping from the waves amazed him. They were, however, he recalled, too fast for him to take pictures of.

In 1945, the dropping of an atomic bomb had completely destroyed Hiroshima. The Second World War had ended with Japan's surrender. Allied forces under American control had occupied Japan, with the Australian Royal Engineers being based at Kure. An American ink stamp on his service record marked Frank's arrival there on 14 May 1953. It was updated on 15 May with 'Taken on Strength R List Korean Theatre'.

Upon reaching the military depot, Frank discovered that its comfy, warm barracks was not going to be housing him and the other 1000 men he'd arrived

A convoy of American GMC trucks crammed with newly arrived British troops and their equipment snaking through the city of Kure. They are passing a tram painted in bottle green.

When the officers disembarked from the ship, they were put onto a bus that travelled in the convoy. The vehicles passed through a checkpoint and across a pontoon bridge.

with. An instructor from the battle camp grumbled at the newly arrived soldiers, 'After six weeks on a troopship you're unfit and no bloody use to anyone.'

Frank and his comrades were immediately ordered to dress and kit up in full combat gear. They endured an all-day, feet-blistering, twenty-five-mile march into the steeply hilled countryside to the battle camp at Hara Mura.

Frank was shocked to find they would be bedding down in sleeping bags in the open among the scrub-covered Japanese hills. These replicated the rough terrain of Korea. Frank and the other new arrivals would have to earn the 'right' to sleep in a tent.

The first morning the new arrivals had to scramble from their sleeping bags, scrub up using cold water, have breakfast and then report for a long day of training.

Training involved:

- Fitness runs in which the international mix of regiments competed to outdo each other.
- Learning how to survive in the wild by living off the land. The instructor said to Frank, 'If it scuttles, slithers or runs it's dinner. If you're hungry, you'll eat anything.'

At daybreak, it was a rude awakening from the instructors, who were veterans of the Second World War and Korea.

- How to handle and fire weapons. Lee Enfield .303 rifles fired with a loud crack. The Sten machine-guns rattled while the instructor yelled, 'Short bursts, Frank, short bursts.'
- How to fight in unarmed combat.
- How to walk. Frank was taught to look down to make sure there was no sign of danger. He had to check there were no unexploded munitions, no trip wire linked to a hidden grenade in scrub or a tree, or disturbed earth where a mine was buried. He would need to step forward, look ahead, then left and right for any danger and then down again before taking another pace. After repeating this exercise a hundred times over, he could move automatically without thinking about it and surprisingly quickly through enemy territory. He knew not to touch any object for fear it had been booby-trapped.
- How to tactically advance as part of a unit. Frank learned to stop, take aim and provide covering fire for another man who was to one side and moving forward beyond him. When this comrade stopped to aim and fire, Frank advanced. The theory of the fire and move drill was instilled in the men to avoid a fatal accident.

Combat exercises took place day and night. Frank crawled up steep hills, through natural forests and scrub. He crawled through man-made jungles of barbed wire and mud-filled slit trenches. Live rounds were shot overhead, and bullets spat up the dirt in front of him as mortars thumped nearby, setting the tinderbox scrub ablaze. The instructor shouted at him to move here and shoot that, then move there and grenade that. Frank helped a comrade who had stumbled and was injured. An instructor shouted at him, 'You! Why are you helping that man? If you stop and help the wounded, you're not fighting the enemy and they'll kill you and the man you're helping. Leave him, get going!'

Frank remembered weapons inspection being at random times through the day and night. It was instilled in him to automatically clean his weapon and kit during the day to ensure everything was in working order. He was covered in mud and bleeding from several cuts from crawling under a lattice of barbed wire when he was called to present arms. The instructor said, 'Your boots are laced wrong!' Without question, Frank took them off to be shown how to lace them for jungle warfare.

When on guard duty, Frank was told to keep a lookout among the international mix of troops for 'flash Harry' spivs trading stolen supplies with local black marketers. He was also required to watch for soldiers sneaking out of the camp looking for women in the nearest village to smuggle back in. One night, he discovered a Canadian with, as Frank put it, 'two paid-for wives' in his tent.

It was better that Frank had caught the man and seen off the 'wives', before a certain Second World War veteran found them. As Frank explained, 'This veteran had experienced the savagery of the disbanded Imperial Japanese Army and venomously hated all Japanese. He would have brutally taken it out on the Canadian. A high standard of conduct was always expected when encountering the civilians of Japan and Korea. Anyone who fell foul of that got a beating.'

Frank was posted on guard duty with his comrades.

Chapter 2

Capchong and Kamak-san

Entire villages and towns had been completely destroyed in the Korean War. In some places, not a building was left standing after the artillery bombardment and carpet-bombing of the air campaign. Refugee shanty towns had sprung up in areas that were supposed to be abandoned by civilians. This caused security concerns as bandit-like 'stay behind' NKPA guerrillas were known to infiltrate across the frontline. Operating in five-member units, they hid among and preyed upon civilians when short of food as well as raiding army kitchens and ambushing convoys.

Frank wrote in pencil on the blue cover of the negative album 'Negative Alum [sic] No 7. Capchong.' I couldn't find it on a map and wonder if he'd misheard the name of the town.

The American GMC convoys were tactically spaced out and wouldn't stop on their journeys through war-ravaged Capchong (this was the name Frank gave to the area he passed through, but this may not be accurate). It was a dangerous place to linger. As well as the risk from attack, child thieves were known to climb into the back of moving trucks and throw out cargo to waiting accomplices. The fact the convoys had armed guards in the form of replacement troops temporarily discouraged the gangs. A lone ROKA soldier patrolled the street, walking by the patriotically flown South Korean flags (see right of photograph).

When leaving this shanty town in fading light and deteriorating weather, the convoy travelled on via a firmer road surface stained by tyre tracks and slicks of engine oil. Military-installed telegraph poles lined the side of this road and people went about their daily lives among dilapidated brick buildings that had been pockmarked by shells and bullets. It was grim and dilapidated. Capchong, despite its impoverished look, seemed a safer place to live compared to the ruins on its outskirts.

On 15 June 1953, it was noted on Frank's service record, 'Korea TOS [Taken on Strength] from R List to 28 Field Engineer Regiment.' They were

The trucks passed perilously close to leaning, ramshackle huts built from the planks of old cargo crates. The roofs were ceramic slates, wooden or metal panels, or straw thatched. A chimney was made of old artillery shell casings welded together.

A child's clothing was made from a cut-up uniform, hence the enormous pouches on the front. The children stood by what looks like a polluted river, watching the trucks pass by.

Capchong was a warren of muddy streets and alleyways between packaging-crate-walled lean-to stores and homes.

Regiments from different Commonwealth nations were based on the Kansas Line with the camps stretching over the horizon.

attached to the 29th Infantry Brigade of the 1st Commonwealth Division. It consisted of British, Canadian, Australian and New Zealand artillery, engineers, infantry, tank and logistics regiments. It also included the 60th Indian Field Ambulance Unit, with medical support provided by the Norwegian Mobile Army Surgical Hospital. The 1st Commonwealth Division was part of the US I Corps, which also included the US 1st Cavalry Division, the US 3rd and 25th Infantry Divisions, and the ROKA 1st Division. The Commonwealth Division occupied the strategically important sector of the battlefront on the Jamestown Line that was supported by the various camps of the Kansas Line. The sector stretched from the Kimpo Peninsula beside the Yellow Sea on the west coast to Kumhwa six miles inland. The frontline was just thirty miles from Seoul, the South Korean capital.

55 Field Squadron Royal Engineers ran an engineering school to provide training in field works for rifle companies and assault pioneers newly posted to Korea. The training occurred between the hours of 08:30 and 12:30 or 16:30, depending on what was being taught. It covered bunker building, sandbagging, minefields, booby traps and trip flares. The best advice a sapper gave when teaching about what to do if you found yourself stuck in a minefield and no one was injured was to 'sit down and wait to be rescued'.

Frank joined 3 Troop 55 Field Squadron Royal Engineers who were camped south of the River Imjin.

Frank was billeted in a tent. He obeyed the golden rule of camping, which is not to let your kit touch the side of the tent. To do so would mean when it rained the water would flood into the tent at the contact point, soaking everyone and everything inside. He didn't want to fall foul of the comrades he was sharing a tent with.

Men in the 1950s slicked back their hair by combing in Brylcreem hair cream. This was sold separately to the sappers by the NAAFI (Navy, Army and Air Force Institute) shops. Apart from the South Koreans, British soldiers were the lowest paid. Out of their wages, they had to pay for their personal toiletries, and it was noticed that in Korea a soldier paid more for these than anywhere else in the world. In Korea, a 4oz bar of soap cost 9d, but at British bases in Germany, it cost only 4d. In the 'NAAFI, Korea (Prices)' debate in the House of Commons on Thursday, 22 March 1951, Brylcreem was quoted as being priced in Korea at 1s. and 10d.

Frank's negative album No. 7 was also marked 'Kamak-San walk'. Some of the 1st Commonwealth Division camps on the Kansas Line were at the foot of the gigantic Mount Kamak-san. Rising to 2200 feet, it dominated the surrounding hills and was a key strategic feature in Korea's ancient and modern wars. The 28 Field Engineer Regiment diary stated '12th of November 1953 members of

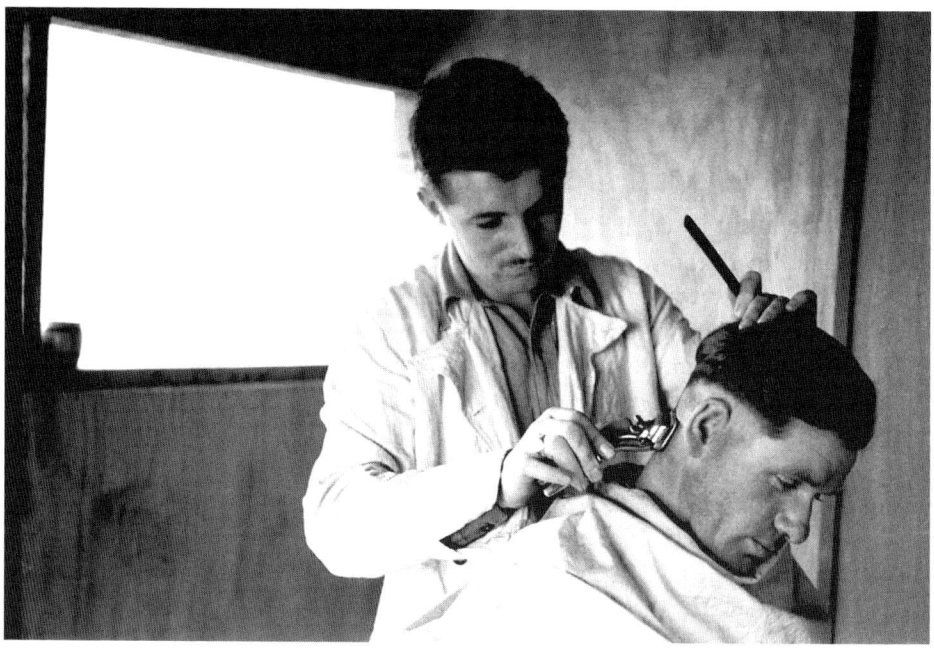

The camp's barber gave his own style of army haircut.

The view from Mount Kamak-san.

the Regimental Headquarters, 12 Field Squadron and 55 Field Squadron have spent the night on Kamak-san. This has enabled the men to get a wider picture of regimental and divisional activities as well as valuable training and installing confidence in cold weather equipment.'

Frank and the other recent arrivals who had reached Korea in June 1953 were considered by the veterans as, 'kids, fresh-faced, green and wet behind the ears'.

To get the new guys quickly used to the terrain, or the 'real Korea' as a sergeant called it, an expedition was organized to take them on a 'walk' up Mount Kamak-san. This in reality was a steep climb. Frank made a second trek in April 1954, himself now leading a group of replacements intended for a number of regiments. The photographs from this second expedition are in colour.

On both expeditions, Frank's party stopped to look back at the jeep track they had traversed. It was a winding maze that had been bulldozed through wild flowers, long grass and scrub. They avoided shortcutting across and through the overgrown, dry paddy fields, which had been abandoned years before because of unexploded mines. These explained the absence of wildlife. Frank stepped into the boot prints of the man ahead of him as the track ended at a treeline masking the rise of the ground. The expedition's point man scouted a potential path, which was

Having made their way partly up Kamak-san, the expedition stopped and looked down and to the west at what had come to be known in Korea as Gloucester Valley.

up and through the dense forest. They followed him past the pits of old forgotten trenches.

Trucks often passed through Gloucester Valley heading to the Kansas Line. Frank recalled when travelling to camp in the back of a truck with his fellow sappers that the banter had suddenly stopped at that point. He said, 'I saw the haunted expression on the face of a returning veteran opposite me as he vividly remembered what had happened there.'

In 1951, 55 Field Squadron Royal Engineers had scouted and constructed roads and cut tracks through the densely forested steep hills to the River Imjin, north of Kamak-san. The 29th British Infantry Brigade had then dug into the Kansas Line. An attached Belgian battalion had crossed to the northern bank of the river by

Above left: *Frank experienced the thickness of the bushy scrub and groves of gangling trees that concealed the craggy, precarious slope he was climbing on Kamak-san.*

Above right: *After the cuts and scrapes sustained from the scrub, the veterans leading Frank's first trek up Kamak-san took the party up a jagged gradient of precarious, sharp gorges. Rock fall had been washed down the mountain by previous monsoon flooding as well as the spring thaw. In places, the men's boots dug into loose strata, but every step had to be carefully considered on a battlefield containing forgotten munitions, along with natural hazards.*

bridges constructed by 55 Field Squadron. On the moonlit night of 22 April 1951, the Chinese People's Liberation Army (PLA) had launched its spring offensive. The Chinese infantry had crossed en masse to the southern banks of the river while under intense artillery bombardment. A detachment of Royal Engineers, with the Royal Ulster Rifles, had crossed the river the opposite way to protect the bridges and support the Belgian battalion. However, the bridge force had been ambushed and had to withdraw south of the river into the hills, while under continuous enemy fire from in front and behind. This had left the Belgian battalion surrounded.

On Monday, 23 April, the PLA had crested hill 257. The Royal Engineers had advanced, with artillery support from Bofors light anti-aircraft guns, and taken back what became known as 'Sapper Hill'.

The Chinese had ascended and flanked across the slopes of Kamak-san to surround and cut off the 1st Battalion Gloucester Regiment. An attempt to reach them had then failed. The 29th Infantry Brigade withdrew as the Royal Engineers advanced in an attempt to recapture the bridges that were now two miles behind Chinese lines. This action allowed the Belgian battalion to withdraw, and the bridges be destroyed by artillery fire.

On 24 April, a second attempt had been made to break through to the then cut-off Gloucester Valley by a Philippine infantry battalion supported by British centurion tanks of the 8th Royal Hussars. American infantry with tank support had then made a third attempt. After three days and nights of intense fighting, on 25 April, the 1st Battalion Gloucester Regiment made a last stand on hill 235. This became known as Gloucester (Gloster) Hill. The few survivors were taken prisoner, but the Chinese offensive had been stopped.

Frank injured his hand on his first trek up Kamak-san. The expedition made Frank and his comrades aware of the need to maintain peak physical fitness. The sappers needed to be ready to undertake mountain operations at short notice to counter an enemy offensive. The exhaustion of the climb across this steep, almost impenetrable terrain set in. Frank recalled, 'It was hard going and almost killed a man, who like me was new, because he wasn't acclimatized to the conditions.'

Above: *Frank said about the dense terrain on Kamak-san, 'One ridge looked very much like another. You'd think you were at the top and then you'd find the ground stretched out into a hidden gorge to go down into. It was a thicket-laced depression with giant weathered boulders obstructing your way. They sapped morale as soon as you saw them, and once across you were glad to be climbing again.'*

Left: *On his second trek, Frank walked through the narrow channels formed by the flood-deposited boulder piles.*

Above: *The expedition looked north towards the River Imjin and beyond the frontline that split Korea into two polar opposite cultures. There was silence as they were far above the battlefield. Frank and his comrades on both expeditions took in the peacefulness of the mountain.*

Right: *At the peak of Kamak-san, a granite monolith that was 170cm tall stood on a rock-pile altar. Frank and his comrades thought it was an old grave. However, this stone was known as a biseok and was called 'Kamak-seon-bi' (now Gamak-seon-bi) or 'Jinheung-wang-sunsu-bi' after the 24th king of the Silla Dynasty.*

The king had placed monoliths, regarded as national treasures, upon mountains to mark his land during the wars of the Three Kingdoms of Korea (57 BC to AD 668). Four of the stones were confirmed to date from his reign, but the engraving on the Kamak-seon-bi were too weathered for its origins to be identified. The stone was also known by the name of 'Bit-dol-dae-wang-bi', meaning Rain Rock King. According to a fable, in ancient times, the stone's original location was in the mountain pass of the village of Hwangbang-ri to the south of Kamak-san. All local travellers knelt and prayed at the stone for safe passage through the mountain pass. Foreigners, oblivious to the custom, passed by the stone without a second thought and many suffered a lethal fate. The local people decided to perform a ritual to the mountain spirit to allow safe passage for all travelling through the pass. The mountain spirit then materialized in people's dreams, requesting the sacrifice of cattle at the stone. On the following day, the cows were stricken with fever and the people who refused to sacrifice their cows died. A traveller then noticed the stone was missing from the mountain pass. It was found to have mysteriously moved to the summit of Kamak-san. The stone remained a hallowed artefact tended to by visiting pilgrims from across Korea until the country was divided in 1945.

On his wanderings from camp, Frank discovered a village west of Kamak-san, where women washed clothes in a mountain stream. The clothing was hung on the bushes to dry.

Capchong and Kamak-san 25

Frank didn't worry that this village was out of bounds to him and wandered around it unarmed, much to the surprise of the locals.

This tranquil hamlet tucked away in the hills seemed frozen in time and not to have physically changed in centuries.

Chapter 3

The Korean People

When an officer called an elderly farmer a 'peasant' Frank felt the officer was being rude, as he believed the farmer to be no different to his own father. Frank said, 'I considered myself to be a guest in Korea. I was willing to abide by their culture and I was determined to see the country as it truly was.'

Frank walked several miles each day when exploring. He filled three of his blue negative albums, pencilling on the covers 'No 8 Packet D', 'No 10 Packet C' and 'No 11 Packet B Juchong'. A fourth album was pencilled 'K1A' and titled in blue fountain pen 'Going to Inchong & Juchong'. The photographs are of the countryside inland of the coastal port of Inchon where the 1st Commonwealth Division had a rest camp. Frank labelled his colour slides 'Inchong'.

Farmers and merchants used a cow and cart to haul goods along powdery, white dust tracks that divided soft-earth farmland or marshy paddy fields. The tracks were too narrow and fragile for motor vehicles and their weight would have caused them to sink into the ground. Often a track was just wide enough for a single cart to use. Frank wondered what would happen if a cart came the opposite way because it would be difficult for the wagons to pass each other.

The Korean People 27

Right: *Frank in Korea in 1953.*

Below: *The absence of tractors and horses in Korea meant it was a cow that ploughed the fields intended for rice farming. This happened as late as June after the harvest of wheat and barley crops.*

Above: *A cow enjoying a good meal of hay at the end of a working day. On its back is a blanket woven from rice straw.*

Left: *A farmer walks along a road scarred with tyre tracks. The heavy buckets are attached to a bamboo pole on a wooden A-frame slung across his back and held in place by straps of plant stems.*

The Korean People 29

The soldiers nicknamed these buckets 'honey pots' for the buzzing flies feasting upon the cow dung that the buckets contained. The farmer spread the dung using it as fertilizer on a ploughed field. Being a farmer's son, Frank was used to the smell.

After being treated with manure, the paddy fields were flooded to turn them into ponds. The rice seedlings were taken from dry beds and planted into the submerged mud a foot apart to allow for growth. The neat rows of vegetation in the swamp-like plantations would continue to be irrigated by the monsoon rain in July.

A typical Korean home was single storey with an external chimney or an out-building on the east or west walls.

The fireplace was outside and built into the stone and mud brick wall on the eastern or western side of the house. A plaster coating prevented erosion by rain and heat damage from the fire. Heat flowing through under-floor pipes warmed the house. It escaped out of the external chimney built on the opposite wall. Frank noticed the chimneys of the newly built homes were made of artillery shell casings welded together. He suspected the under-floor pipes were as well.

The Korean People   31

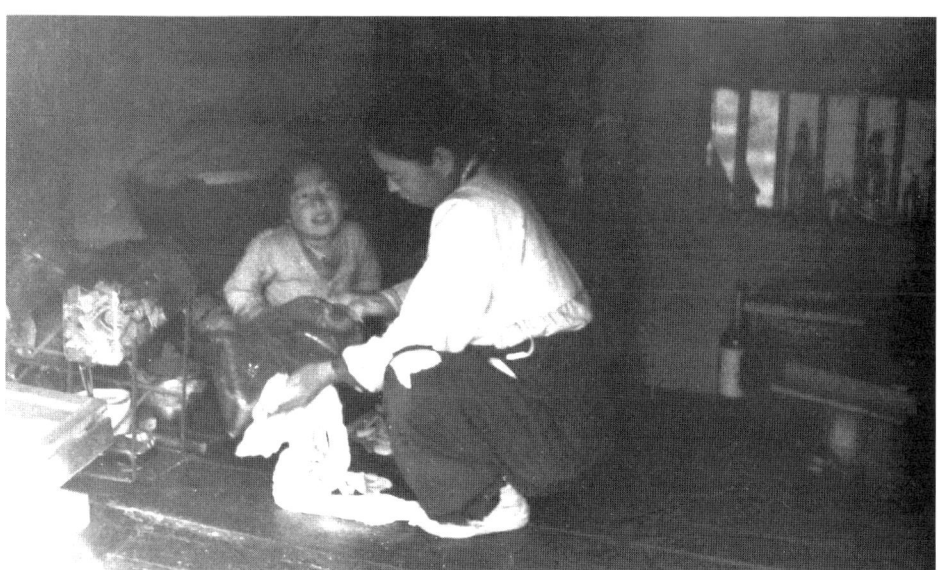

Entering a Korean home was out of bounds to UN soldiers. In summer, the south wall of some houses was wood panelled and removable to stop a home from overheating. Frank, standing outside, asked for permission to take a picture by pointing to his camera.

On laundry day, a pot and wooden tubs were used to wash clothes at a nearby water source. The water was wrung out of the clothing by hand. The washing was laid out to dry on the scrub in the hot sun.

Above left: *The family laundry was taken home.*

Above right: *A wooden A-frame was used to carry the washtubs home.*

Left: *As this woman walks home, the heavy-looking head basket was full of groceries, as was the bag in a sling on her back.*

The Korean People 33

#

Above left: *A mother carries her baby on her back in a sling.*

Above right: *Frank said, 'To get anywhere it was by Shanks's pony. A traveller had to walk, no matter how far it was.' The Petrol, Oil and Lubricant (POL) pipeline, seen in the background of the photograph, seemed like a modern intrusion into this ancient land.*

Children were curious when they saw Frank as a lone, unarmed soldier with a smile and a camera walking along the road.

Left: *A boy and girl at Juchong.*

Below: *Frank titled this photograph a 'Korean Homestead'. It is possible that because of the size of the room and the dozen children present it was actually a school.*

The Korean People   35

A wooden plank on a bump of dirt to make a seesaw was a common sight, and it was surprising how high in the air it catapulted the smaller children.

Frank was attracted to a village shop in the same way he had been by the one back home in Chalk. Although this Korean store had papers and magazines in a different language, he found chocolate bars were an international commodity. When a packaging crate was finished with it became part of an external wall.

Left: *Frank said, 'A storekeeper had everything you needed. If he didn't have it, you didn't need it. Even battlefield salvage was for sale.'*

Below: *Mounds and statues lined a hillside burial ground. A solitary gardener cared for the park-like slope.*

The Korean People 37

The statues were gigantic stone guardians known as Muninseok that protected the tombs of the burial ground from evil spirits.

The Muninseok were sculpted as robed courtiers clutching symbolic objects known as Hols. A Hol was shown to the court when the King had given a nobleman permission to address him. Muninseok had been placed to guard tombs since the Silla kingdom of 57 BC to AD 935. It was a tradition introduced by the

Frank visited a Buddhist temple at Inchon.

Chinese Tang dynasty, which continued through to the Korean Joeson dynasty. It ended in 1910 with the invasion by Japan. During the occupation, looters shipped numerous Muninseok to Japan. This both encouraged resistance fighters and, it was said, angered the spirits to vengeance. Frank noticed two of the Muninseok facing each other like rival chess pieces. It felt like a symbol of politically divided 1950s Korea.

Above left: *A priest helped children to climb a tree in the temple courtyard.*

Above right: *Frank observed people arriving to pray at the temple.*

Opposite: *Inside the temple, Frank was impressed by the intricately painted décor. The paintings of haloed figures were on canvases made of silk scrolls. The statues were bronze and surrounded by bouquets of freshly cut flowers. This and the exquisite detail of the ceiling made visiting the temple one of the highlights of his time exploring Korea.*

Left: *After the monsoon season, the rice plants had grown to a sufficient height for the paddy fields to be drained. This created a dry environment in which the rice continued to grow. Any repair work required to the walls of the fields was carried out while the paddy fields were free of water.*

Below: *October was when the rice was harvested. For an elderly farmer, it was exhausting and dangerous work in which his hands or fingers could be cut off or a leg fatally slashed by a slip of the razor-sharp sickle.*

The Korean People   41

Above left: *A common sight was a farmer with an A-frame laden with an enormous and heavy straw bale.*

Above right: *Frank found that most people he met, like this elderly gentleman, showed generous hospitality to a father's son far from home.*

Chapter 4

The River

On the rust-marked and stapled cream cover of a negative album, someone had typed, 'Negative Holder. Ref No: – … Subj: – … Type: – …' Frank had written in pencil in these fields: 'K3a', 'Korean River' and 'Bridging, Misc.'.

Building a Bailey floating bridge was an experience that stayed with him. He recalled hearing the metal girders squeal as they were manually hauled into position and bolted into place with a ringing crash of hammers. He felt an enormous sense of accomplishment when a bridge he was working on was completed.

During the monsoon and floods of the spring thaw, the River Imjin quickly swelled to 40 feet in depth and 1000 feet in width. The rushing current was able to propel the debris of rock boulders and 12-inch icebergs at incredible speed. These could slam into and destroy the sturdiest-looking bridge.

The assembly of a Bailey bridge was essential training, to allow for quick deployment or recovery in combat operations. It was a vital skill in Korea, where many bridges could be destroyed in a single flood.

Frank said, 'To be a sapper, at some point you had to build a bridge. Everyone pitched in.'

Donald Bailey and the staff of the Experimental Bridging Establishment had invented the Bailey bridge in 1941, during the Second World War. It comprised easily assembled panels that were bolted together to the length required. If needed, additional trusses could provide extra strength, allowing the bridge to support a weight of up to 70 tons.

On 22 June 1953, the flood precaution plan Operation Amazon was introduced. It set out the instructions for sappers to clean debris away from the bridge sites. It was suggested that the 1st Royal Tank Regiment provide a tank to smash up any large mass of debris. Cableways were to be established by the sappers as a means of providing an emergency crossing should a bridge be damaged and washed away. Also, ferries were to operate but only when the floodwater was low enough to avoid a ferry being damaged by debris.

On 25 June, the 901st Pontoon Bridge Company, 1103 Engineer Combat Group (ROKA) discovered a log raft lodged against the float of their bridge. On top of the raft were eight Chinese wooden anti-tank mines. The logs had been stapled together with metal straps and lashed with wire. The weight of the mines had fortunately submerged the raft and the water had extinguished the time fuse. This had saved the bridge.

In summer, the River Imjin was shallow and slow moving. Boats operated from the granular beaches.

Boat '51-157' had been stencilled in paint, 'property processed for export'. The rope mooring partially obscured the month when it was cleared for export from the UK, so it read, '16 Ma... 53'.

'*Corporal Newson of 55 Field Squadron gets his hand in on a nineteen-foot powerboat.*' This was the caption of Frank Merritt's only known published photograph taken in the summer of 1953. It featured in the February 1954 issue of the Royal Engineers in-house magazine The Kansas Tract, Journal of the Royal Engineers. This magazine was published and distributed among the sappers serving in Korea in 1954 and had a life span of only a few issues. A rare copy is exhibited in the Royal Engineer Museum at Gillingham, Kent, open on the page of this photograph.

Left: *On the 50-feet-high riverbank above the floodwater line and with the bank acting as a windbreak were scattered ramshackle huts. They had canvas roofs weighed down with sandbags, and the walls were made from the wooden planks of packaging crates.*

Below: *Korean parents dressed their children in spotless white clothes, but away from maternal eyes, these soon got dirty as the kids playfully foraged for wildlife.*

The River   47

Right: *The shoeshine boy hung around the camp and was assumed to be an orphan. He polished boots so well they surpassed the standards that would have been expected by a parade-ground sergeant.*

Below: *At the camp, these young boys were willing to do odd jobs in exchange for a meal. They peeled a huge pile of potatoes for the sappers' dinner.*

Potato peeling was a job a sergeant usually allocated as a punishment to soldiers. Frank observed, 'It left your fingers shrivelled and sore but attention to detail was required. If you lost too much of a spud when peeling it, then you had to peel more of them, and your mates blamed you for the size of the spuds they got for dinner.'

The Korean boys had the skill of sculptors as they shaved the skins off the potatoes. It was because they wanted to keep this employment and earn a portion of decent-sized roast potatoes to eat. The sappers became father figures to the boys, making sure they were fed and clothed. If they were orphans, this prevented them from being recruited for subversive training by the NKPA as reported in the Monthly Security Intelligence Report of July 1953. With the sappers looking out for the boys, it meant unlike others they were not stealing food or risking death from a stray 'pirate' mine when 'mud larking' on the riverbank for whatever they could catch to eat.

The potatoes sizzled in the roasting tray on the stove of the sappers' field kitchen.

Right: *Frank said, 'There were two things that never changed about army food. One was looking forward to a slap-up meal. The other was being disappointed with what was slapped down on your plate. However, to me, the food always tasted good.'*

Below: *On the southern side of the Imjin, there were scattered ramshackle huts, similar to those found closer to the riverbank, and seen in an earlier picture.*

At the camp on a rest day, for recreation and to maintain fitness, the sappers played football. The 12 Field Squadron put together a team to play other regiments.

Chapter 5

Korean Service Corps

Frank had created a second, blue-cover negative album – 'No. 10', and this was titled 'Sappers At Work'.

The Korean Service Corps was an unarmed jack-of-all-trades auxiliary navvy force made up of conscripts who had failed the ROKA fitness and medical tests.

Korean Service Corps 51

Above: *More than 1000 KSC labourers worked for and alongside the Royal Engineers. Frank said, 'You could ask them to do any job, no matter how dirty and unpleasant, and they were willing to give it a go and they did it well. They were quick learners with an aptitude for engineering. We looked upon them as fellow sappers.'*

Right: *Supplies to the KSC were haphazard and their clothing came from a number of sources. Reversible camouflage jackets, white for a snowy background on one side and brown for mud on the other, were scavenged from the enemy – the PLA or the NKPA. Some uniforms were issued by ROKA, such as the officer's uniform in the photograph with its white arm stripes. Other clothing was American-issue or hand-me-downs donated by the sappers.*

Although it wasn't officially confirmed, some of the KSC were suspected of actually being North Korean or Chinese. When screened by field security, it was discovered that most of the KSC servicemen had no political affiliation. Their loyalty was to their labourer comrades working alongside them. Only the KSC really knew who was from where because of the variation in regional accent.

The KSC regiments had their own officers, and the units attached to 55 Field Squadron reported to their assigned British corporals for work. The KSC officers paid their men erratically on a first-come, first-served basis. The currency was doled out from cash bags, and the money was never counted beforehand, so the last in line often went unpaid. Frank often heard a Korean phrase that sounded to him like, 'Chop-Sum-Ni-Gee.' This was aimed at their officers, and he asked an English-speaking KSC what the translation was. The Korean replied, 'It means you're a big dick, but you're okay, Johnny.'

Frank remembered, 'They invited me to dinner, so I went and had a meal with them. Afterwards, I promised myself I'd never eat what I'd thought was fried snake again.' At the age of 73, he had a flashback to that moment when served dinner at home. He asked me what the strips of meat were and misheard 'fried steak' as 'snake'.

Frank recalled that in 1953, he and his Royal Engineer comrades and the Korean Service Corps were trucked north of the River Imjin to the battlefront of the Jamestown Line. When the trucks couldn't go any further because of rough

The KSC lived separately in the camp. Their food supply was as erratic as their pay and clothing, so the sappers spared some of their rations for them.

After dinner, the pans and mess tins were washed spotlessly clean.

terrain, the sappers and the KSC went on foot up into the fortified hills. The KSC carried heavy loads that were larger than them, consisting of food, water, fuel and munitions, on A-frames on their backs. Working in teams, they manhandled huge timber and concrete joists for miles across mountainous terrain that was inaccessible by vehicle. To Frank, the irony was that the KSC men had been rejected from ROKA for being unfit and second-rate.

Frank said,

> 'We went up at night and arrived at the foot of the slope of a hill. We went inside and up through the tunnels. The sappers and the KSC had hollowed out the hill to turn it into an impregnable fortress. We came out on the other side, below the crest of the hill. Our job was to repair the trenches and bunkers, and we had very little cover to work in. The KSC dragged the timber and concrete across the recently abandoned, obstacle-strewn battlefield. The first time I heard artillery fire, I was scared, but a veteran told me to relax – it was outgoing. We both felt sorry for whoever was on the receiving end of that lot.'

Chinese loudspeakers broadcast music, propaganda and direct appeals for Commonwealth soldiers to surrender. Frank spoke little of the battle that then took place. It was too horrific for him to put into words, though he did recollect hearing the strangled screams of bugles as waves of Chinese soldiers charged uphill. He also mentioned the whole night glowing orange as the slopes became awash with napalm fire. 'It was a nasty way to leave this world,' he said, recalling,

> 'We were ordered back into the tunnels because the trenches were being overrun. This was despite the barbed-wire roofs we'd strung over the top to make it more difficult for them to get in. Our own artillery had been ordered to clear the trenches by using variable time fuse shells. They were going to explode in mid-air and rain dismembering shrapnel down on the enemy. We grabbed and dragged any of either side's wounded who were close to us into the shelter of our tunnels. It didn't matter if they were friend or foe – it was just grab and go. We pulled the men to safety with hardly a moment to spare. I was at the tunnel entrance and given only a lump of timber to use as a weapon. The order was to bash the brains in of anyone who came in after me.'

Chinese infantry were known to use an unstable bomb made of a cloth bag with TNT explosive and a stick grenade inside it. They also used an explosive-tipped spear called a pole charge.

Reliving this time in his nightmares decades later, Frank would call out 'Hey' to a figure who had entered the tunnel and collapsed beside him. He hadn't known if this man was a Chinese or North Korean soldier or a KSC labourer. The man's eyes had been bloodshot, his hair plastered to his scalp by grime that matched the filth on his face and his stained, ragged clothing. Frank had realized that he himself also looked like this and that this stranger was of a similar age. Youthful innocence was a ghostly memory for both of them, and a desperate night of survival had aged them both. Frank never discovered what happened to this man he had sat with in the tunnel. 'He was gone by morning. All he wanted was to get into cover, and all I wanted was to sit on the sheltered, reverse slope of the hill and see the sunrise.'

Casualties among the KSC were shockingly high. ROKA and KSC men who were taken prisoner hardly ever returned home. They were sent to North Korean mining camps on the Chinese border. Eventually, as a reward for years of hard labour, they were granted North Korean citizenship and encouraged to marry. However, their families were for generations stigmatized and discriminated against as foreigners and enemies of the state. They would never improve their social standing from being second from the bottom in North Korean society. Beneath them was only the hated lowest class of political prisoner.

Chapter 6

'Scheme 1'

Frank had titled in pencil the blue covers of three negative albums: 'No Scheme 1', 'No Scheme 2' and 'No Scheme 3'. I could find no records of these operations in the 28 Field Engineer Regiment's diaries of 1953–54. The 'Scheme 1' negatives were cut into strips of three photographs.

Above left: *Captain Edward Sharp, the commanding officer of 3 Troop 55 Field Squadron, used a No. 19 wireless set in his jeep. At the time, wireless radios consisted of fragile electrical valve components. If they came loose or were broken, the radio wouldn't work. Captain Sharp was proficient in keeping his wireless set operational, as previously he had been a regimental signals officer in Korea.*

Above right: *Wanting his jeep to remain mobile, Captain Sharp didn't deploy his No. 2 pattern camouflage netting that would have hidden it while parked.*

Underneath the netting, an officer's jeep contained what was known as a 'Bluebell' kit for mine clearance work. There was also a battlefield first-aid kit as officers were expected to rescue minefield casualties. Captain Sharp had modified his jeep with a layer of sandbags both in the footwells and underneath the seats to take the force of a blast from a buried exploding mine.

The sappers draped camouflage net over their parked truck to break up its distinctive shape and hide it. All vehicles carried properly scrimmed camouflage nets. As the seasons changed, the scrim was altered, so the nets continued to match the surrounding foliage.

The sappers parked their trucks below the crest of the ridge, so as not to be silhouetted against the skyline and in clear view of the enemy. Camouflage netting blended the trucks into the surrounding terrain and prevented light reflecting off the windscreens and windows. Once their vehicles were hidden, the sappers backtracked several metres to disguise any tyre marks that would have given their position away.

In this photograph, the Bren gun has its bipod to keep it off the ground. A sapper's pack and helmet prop up a Lee Enfield .303 rifle. However, other rifles have been carelessly discarded in the dirt. If one of these rifles had been mishandled when picked up, it could have killed a comrade. Sometimes rifles lost by other units were discovered by chance. In a case Frank mentioned, the army dentist returned a rifle to a grateful soldier. It was fortunate he had found it rather than an enemy soldier on the battlefield.

Captain Sharp kept his maps and transparent overlays of troop positions in a wooden case to prevent them from flapping around and reflecting, causing 'shine' that might alert the enemy. He also had a whistle, which was a simple but proven means of communication to rally troops in combat. In the First World War, Frank's father had crawled across the battlefields of France towards the shrill of an officer's whistle.

Above: *A pump was used to obtain water from a river.*

Left: *The collected water was stored in canvas tanks. The sappers used a testing kit to discover the extent of purification needed to kill off waterborne diseases. Debilitating sickness could reduce a company's fighting strength by 20 per cent within twenty-four to forty-eight hours. Water was disinfected with iodine tablets, by drops of chlorine bleach or by boiling. The efforts of sappers to supply water for drinking and hygiene were greatly appreciated by all ranks of the army.*

A D7 Bulldozer was used to cut jeep tracks to increase mobility for general movement or outflank and counter any advancing enemy. The surrounding rugged terrain would hide the tracks until used. These tracks were given codenames for easy use. The Royal Engineers in-house magazine 'Kansas Tract' stated, 'the tracks were called after girls' names and many of the bulldozers after boys' ones. It caused a few interesting situations when reports were passed over the airwaves.'

Fitted to the rear of the bulldozer was the barrel-shaped Hyster D7N 15-ton towing winch. This was operated when the bulldozer was stationary to maximize engine power and, therefore, its pulling strength. The bulldozer's serial number, '88ZX83', may indicate it was fitted with a D-8800 four-cylinder 80hp 13.617cc liquid-cooled diesel engine.

From 1938, three American companies, the Cleveland Tractor Company, Allis-Chalmers International and Caterpillar Inc., had initially all manufactured the 7½-ton medium dozer. During the Second World War, it had been so popular among military engineers globally that orders had surpassed Caterpillar Inc.'s production capability. A licence had then been issued to American Car and Foundry to meet the increasing demand.

The steep hills of Korea and the seasonal weather meant tank warfare and great clashes of armour didn't take place as they had done in the Second World War. Armour brigades found their signals blocked by the mountainous terrain. In winter, the icy slopes restricted massed mobility, and in summer, the vast

The Centurion tank was garaged in camouflage netting mounted on poles to allow it to quickly become mobile again. Foraged vegetation, such as long grass and branches, was laid on the tank to merge it into the landscape. The tank was hull down in the cover of a dried-up flood channel. Its gun turret had a clear line of sight over the rising ground, so it was ready in ambush to snipe at the enemy.

Close to the camouflaged tank, the smell of cooking betrayed its position when dinner was served.

The non-conductive wire poles from an officer's jeep's mine clearance 'Bluebell' kit were used to sweep the road. Probes at a forty-five-degree angle were gently stroked into the road surface rather than pushed in.

ocean-like marshes of paddy fields became unintentional anti-tank traps. The sappers created positions on the forward slopes of the hills of the frontline for the tanks to occupy at night, where they could fire upon the attacking enemy. The tanks withdrew from the frontline before sunrise to occupy individual points where they could take up sniper positions they could use during the day.

Frank didn't know what had been spotted that had betrayed recent enemy activity on this road. The NKPA 'stay behind' guerrillas could have dropped military papers or left a weapon on the ground. It could even have been food waste or a discarded Soviet-brand cigarette butt that had given them away. Intelligence Summary 303, issued on 20 July 1953, reported that on route 33, a box containing twenty detonators for Soviet F1 and RG42 grenades was found.

Wooden box mines were barely detectable unless a sniffer dog was available that could smell the TNT explosive inside. The mines were cheap to make in various sizes and mass-produced. Stability depended on the quality of the wooden casing, as it would rot away in the ground, causing the mine to eventually explode. Some mines had a wooden pressure plate that snapped if the weight of a vehicle or person was applied. Other mines had a safety pin that was pushed out of the fuse

Left: *Between tyre tracks, the probe struck an object buried in the road, and a metal detector was used to investigate.*

Below: *The metal detector didn't find anything. Cautiously, earth was swept away from whatever was buried. An observer in the cover of a ditch kept watch (top left of photograph).*

Above left: *A hinged wooden box was unearthed in the road. This was a Chinese landmine with the only metal parts being the hinge plates and screws.*

Above right: *A dog and handler of 64 Field Park Squadron Royal Engineers.*

by a person or vehicle's weight pressing upon the mine. In either circumstance, this would cause detonation.

The mine could be booby trapped with a hidden second fuse. Alternatively, and more simply, a second mine could be hidden underneath the first to explode both if the first mine was moved. Mindful of this, the corporal fixed a hook attached to a long line to the mine and retreated to the cover of the ditch. Keeping his head down and against the ditch wall, he slowly dragged it from its hole. When the mine didn't explode, he went and made it safe by making sure the pin stayed in place.

Another form of anti-personnel mine reported in Commonwealth Intelligence Brief 1017/1 Appendix K was the Soviet F1 fragmentation grenade that the Chinese encased in a clump of mud. The dry mud shell was inconspicuous on the ground. It was easily kicked or stepped on, causing the mud to break, the grenade's safety spoon to separate and the grenade to explode. The only way to detect these 'mud' mines was by a dog sniffing out the explosive inside.

Thousands of mines were strewn (and still remain) throughout South and North Korea. Mine clearance in the south to free up troop and tank movement was one of the many jobs of the Royal Engineers. The mine clearance dogs proved themselves invaluable, as did the patrol dogs. These canine guards worked best on cold, dry nights because they didn't like heat and rain. A dog would silently stop with ears and nose pointed forward in the direction of the enemy to warn of an ambush. An artillery strike would then be accurately called in by the patrol. With the ambush site destroyed, the patrol would resume with the lead scout preceding the dog as it was susceptible to trip wires. On one patrol, a tunnel linking back to the enemy line was discovered and it was scheduled for explosive demolition.

The Royal Australian Engineers and the 3rd Battalion Royal Australian Regiment recognized just how effective the dogs were. The British Sappers of Dog Troop 64 Field Park Squadron assisted them with the training of their dogs. The Australians nicknamed their patrol dogs 'Land Sharks' because of their temperament. However, a German shepherd dog called Bruce who had a pure white coat didn't mind the British Sappers camouflaging him by staining him in a bath of cold coffee to protect him from snipers.

When laying a minefield, a permanent landmark that would not be changed by battle or the weather was recorded as a reference point on a map. However, the wrong feature might be recorded, and the position of the mines would become lost. They were then known as 'pirate mines'. Frank's experience was that no matter how accurate the records of where the UN had laid mines, with warning signs in different languages, symbols and perimeter fences, the mines shifted in the ground with the changing of the weather. He explained, 'Rain pushed up the water table as the ground flooded and swelled into a muddy porridge. The mines moved in landslides or were washed away to become lost.' The 12 Field Squadron Royal Engineers had written in the war diary on 2 May 1953, 'mines practically washed out by flooding of the river'.

Frank said of pirate mines that, 'The odd one would turn up indiscriminately to murder friend, foe or civilian – usually kids. Mines are crude and cause carnage. They should be banned.'

Chapter 7

'Scheme 2'

The sappers camouflaged their Bedford QLR signals truck and their QL office truck, plus the support vehicles that formed a mobile HQ. If they needed to, they could remove the netting and be on the move again very quickly. The Bedford QL series of trucks were manufactured for use by the British armed forces in the Second World War.

Wireless security frequencies for high-frequency sets were changed monthly, with all stations re-netting to their new frequency at the time stated in standing orders. Net control sets were set up using a wavemeter to zero in on the frequency. A tolerance of 0.02 per cent on either side of the frequency was authorized. The accuracy of a wavemeter was regularly tested by the security troop at the Signals Command Group. In addition to maintaining secure communications, an operator kept the batteries of the Nos. 19, 31, 62 and 88 sets charged. He knew the type and

Only the high-frequency radio whip antennas of the vehicles remained visible. The aerials overcame the natural signal-jamming effect of the Korean hills on the very-high-frequency radio sets.

Quick-fire messages broadcast from other units had to be clearly understood to adapt to any rapidly changing situation. The enemy intercepted and frequently interrupted transmissions by broadcasting fake messages. Although the enemy's voice procedure was deceptively good, their English language sounded too perfect. They spoke without the regional accents most of the soldiers possessed. An operator was rarely fooled when listening to the voices on the busy regimental net and able to pick out the real messages for their units.

operational ranges of the radio sets he had issued to even the farthest detachment on the regimental net. This ensured a twenty-four-hour communications link to the most remote unit.

The sappers would arrange a time to join the net of the regiment whose area of control they would be working in and vice versa. For example, on 1 June 1953, 12 Field Squadron contacted 2 Royal Australian Regiment at 17:10 hours to arrange to join their wireless net at 24:00 hours. This was before the sappers commenced night work on the Bowling Alley Road.

Right: *The troop officer held the British Army rank of second lieutenant. It was important for officers and operators to be highly skilled in wireless operation due to the mix of international units the sappers worked with.*

Below: *Rifles were stacked against each other to form a pyramid to keep them off the ground as the sappers worked digging a gun pit.*

The sappers used Bedford QLD series four-wheel-drive trucks for transports.

Working as a radio operator, Frank was dispatched to a grid reference in a Willys jeep (designed and manufactured by Willys-Overland Motors from the Second World War onwards) fitted with a No. 19 wireless. Upon arrival at his destination, he broadcast a situation report back to the signals truck. Frank kept to the wireless procedure using the channel and call sign he had been briefed upon. The operator recognized Frank's distinctive rasping voice and his regional accent.

Bedford army trucks were generally 19-feet long, 70-feet wide and 10 feet in height. Their maximum road speed was 38 miles per hour, but in Korea, the speed limit was 15 miles per hour because of the precarious conditions of the dirt roads. The truck had a solitary driver with an escape hatch in the top of the cab on the passenger side. The truck wasn't armoured, and the back was covered in a retractable canvas skin. The QLD general service cargo truck was the most common type. It was able to carry up to eleven passengers or three tons in weight and variants existed as mobile kitchens, machinery workshops, etc. The QLR was a signals variant that the sappers also used.

Above: *Sappers were perched on the top of a Bedford truck as it drove by.*

Right: *Often a 'young officer' was posted to the field squadron for 'regimental duty to acquire a background of practical experience'. This was the second stage in their training course, the first being eighteen weeks' tuition in basic field engineering at the School of Military Engineering Chatham, England. All sappers found Korea was a constant engineering challenge, throwing up problems never encountered before.*

70   The Royal Engineers in Korea: The Photographic Memoir of Frank Merritt

A Bedford truck has stopped in bushes and its netting has been pulled over it.

The sappers camouflaged their Morris 15-CWT truck.

The Morris 15-CWT truck was designed and manufactured by the British Morris Commercial Cars company. The General Service cargo body averaged 13-feet long and 6-feet wide, with a maximum road speed of 40 miles per hour. The CS8 version was produced from 1934 to 1941 and was a two-wheel-drive, two-axle light truck. The first production run of trucks had open cabs with a small glass plate windbreak mounted in front of the driver and canvas roll-up doors. Later models were equipped with full windscreens and metal half doors. The CS8 was used by all military services and was exported to Commonwealth nations. The enemy, the Chinese People's Liberation Army, were known to use Morris trucks in Korea, having been supplied with them by the British during the Second World War to deploy against Japan.

A Dodge WC-51 ¾-ton 4×4 all-terrain vehicle passes the sappers' camouflaged positions. From this photograph, it is not clear who the occupants of the vehicle are. The paint is chipped and there is a faded small star and English numbering on the bumper.

The WC-51 and its twin, the WC-52, were nicknamed 'Beeps', which stood for big jeeps. Dodge Fargo USA manufactured them from 1942 to 1945. During the Second World War, they were used worldwide as open-topped weapon carriers mounted with heavy machine guns or as a ten-man squad transport. The WC-51 was 13-feet long, 6-feet wide and 5 feet in height, or 6 feet if given a canvas roof. A Dodge T-214 six-cylinder petrol engine powered it. The US government had exported 10,884 to Britain, 24,902 to the Red Army of the Soviet Union and more than 3711 to China. The British had additionally supplied the Kuomintang forces (the Chinese nationalist army) to fight the Japanese occupation during the Second World War. As the People's Liberation Army had won the Chinese Civil War, both UN forces and the enemy used the WC-51 and WC-52 in Korea.

This patrol was a four-man reconnaissance unit.

A recon patrol operated behind enemy lines for up to thirty-six hours at a time, with orders not to engage the enemy. The patrol searched for well-camouflaged enemy positions. Having surveyed enemy movement, the patrol would radio for an artillery bombardment to destroy the entire location.

The patrol was armed with Short Magazine Lee Enfield (SMLE) Mk 3 rifles. It was a single, bolt-action rifle and Frank's father had been armed with an earlier version in the First World War. The British Army rifle had hardly changed since 1895. It had been named after the designer of the bolt system, James Paris Lee, and its place of manufacture, the Royal Small Arms Factory in Enfield. The SMLE Mk 3 averaged 44 inches in length and fired a .303 cartridge that was loaded one round at a time. A ladder magazine of five to ten rounds was used for rapid fire. After each round was fired, the bolt was pulled to eject the spent casing. A rifleman was able to exceed the sergeant's order of, 'Five rounds – rapid fire.'

The soldiers were capable of what was known as the 'mad minute', in which they could fire a minimum of twenty rounds. During the First World War, German troops reported the failure of an infantry charge due to British machine gun fire. In fact, it had been British soldiers armed with Lee Enfield rifles. Australian, Canadian, Belgian and Luxembourg soldiers also used Lee Enfield rifles in Korea.

64 Field Park Squadron used a combination of available tractor units and tank transport trailers to ferry their heavy plant machinery. This trailer had jack-knifed on a narrow S-bend of a road and its cargo of an NCK 304 crane-shovel-excavator had toppled into the road's drainage ditch.

The crane's serial number was '01BY04' and 'Bassoon' had also been painted on it. Local boys were fascinated by the size of the fallen crane.

A lone sapper was left to wait for the recovery team to come and try to disentangle this mess of trailer and crane, with its earth shovel, coiled draglines and camouflage netting. A boy in a cut-down uniform was thrilled to wear the hat of the sapper.

In the Korean War collection at the Imperial War Museum, there is an uncredited photograph of the Royal Engineers quarrying stone for road repair using the NCK 304 crane, serial number 'O1BY05'. In the IWM photograph, the NCK 304 signage was visible on the chassis and boom of the crane, so that image allowed me to identify the crashed crane '01BY04' in Frank's photograph.

NCK stood for Newton Chambers Koehring. They were a subsidiary of Newton Chambers and Co Ltd of Sheffield, UK. After the Second World War, its factory had switched back from the manufacture of battle tanks to producing crane-shovel-excavators for rebuilding work. In 1947, NCK had been formed, upon agreement with Koehring Company of Milwaukee, Wisconsin, USA to re-engineer the Koehring 304 for production using UK parts. Both the US and the UK version of the 304 are still in operation today.

The sappers set up temporary water points (known as 'WPs') when the permanent WPs were shut down. The Royal Engineers diary stated that on 18 November 1953 the Pintail WP was closed at 18:00 hours as the water was contaminated with diesel. The wooden water towers were emptied, and the sappers climbed in and scrubbed them out with soap. On 15 December 1953, the water was contaminated again by diesel flowing downstream from a broken pipeline across the River Hantan in the ROKA sector. US Army Engineers repaired the pipeline. On 28 February 1954, the spring thaw caused sediment problems, and on 1 March, the water was too muddy to drink until 16:06 hours.

Camouflage netting hid this temporary water point. The water was filtered through a purification plant and pumped into canvas storage tanks. The supply of drinkable water to a thirsty army was a main priority of the sappers, with tens of thousands of gallons needed per day.

The chipped and faded stencilled paintwork identified the water bowser as having once belonged to a US Army Division based at Inchon.

Two slices of white bread and a cup of tea improved the dinner of meat stew. Above this sergeant's stripes was the blue shield and red crown patch of the 1st Commonwealth Division.

Chapter 8

'Scheme 3'

The Army Bell Model 47D H-13B 'Sioux' helicopter became the iconic symbol of the Korean War. The helicopter was primarily used in the rapid evacuation of the wounded from a combat zone by flying over the steep hills and paddy fields that were impassable to ambulances. The alternative method to get an injured soldier to hospital was by placing a casualty on a stretcher in a jeep and attempting to drive through the rough maze of tracks cut by a bulldozer. It was a long, hazardous journey that risked further injury to the casualty. Worse still, in the summer, the 'ambulance' jeep kicked up a fog of dust that attracted enemy artillery fire. Because of this, the jeep evacuated personnel at night and in bad weather as the helicopter could only fly during the daytime and in fair weather conditions. Two stretchers bearing casualties were strapped on either side of the helicopter's bubble cockpit and then flown to the American and Norwegian Mobile Army Surgical Hospitals.

The 'Sioux' helicopter was a three-seat aircraft flown by American pilots. Royal Engineers flew as observers for the daily reconnaissance of Korea's fragile road system. Weather damage caused potholes and cracks, and vehicle wheels could destroy a road by crumbling it into a fine powder or a muddy quagmire. A sapper in a helicopter was able to quickly report where immediate repairs were needed. Another aerial reconnaissance role for the sappers was surveying potential routes for troop movement.

With his Lee Enfield rifle cradled in his arms, this sapper stood in the escape hatch of the truck's cab as his convoy approached a town.

The convoy rolled through a town bustling with soldiers from different nations and civilians going about their daily lives.

The vehicles on the convoy were well spaced as it travelled a narrow road through drained paddy fields, where farmers weeded the crops and fought insect infestations. The wheels of the vehicles ahead were ploughing up the road into a fog of dust as they approached the river bridge.

Carrying a detachable water tanker, this Bedford truck was parked on the river estuary. The sappers were unloading their equipment to set up a temporary water point.

Above: *The camouflaged Bedford trucks were parked hull-down in the cover of the embankment. The bare-chested sapper has spotted something moving in his kit as it lay on the ground.*

Left: *Finding a snake, the sapper showed it to his mates and asked, 'Is it poisonous?'*

When the sappers found a snake, they studied its colour and markings. Most likely they had not yet attended the snake lecture in which the advice was not to handle a snake and if they disturbed one to just let it slither away. Frank hated snakes and left the sappers to deal with it.

The Bren gun was a light machine gun named after Brno, the city in Czechoslovakia where Václav Holek of the Zbrojovka Brno Factory had designed it in 1935. It was originally named the ZGB 33 and was a direct descendent of the Czechoslovak ZB VZ .26 light machine gun. Various British companies obtained licences to manufacture the Bren gun for the British Army. It had a lower pistol grip and included a forward mount for a bipod or a tripod. The gun was recognizable by its top-mounted, sickle-shaped, 30-round box magazine. The Bren gun fired the standard .303 cartridge and the ZB VZ fired a 56mm Mauser round. The Bren was gas-operated, with the propellant released from an exhaust near the muzzle through a controller that had four adjustment holes of different sizes. This was to regulate the gas expulsion, so the gun would work at different environmental temperatures. The colder the climate, the more gas was vented for the gun to operate. It was able to fire a maximum of 540 rounds per minute, with the spent cartridges ejecting downwards out of the gun. The Bren gunner fired in five-round bursts and, to prevent jamming, usually loaded the magazine with just twenty-eight rounds. After ten magazines were used, the hot barrel was changed. The gun crew carried spare barrels and swapped out the used barrel by a release

A sapper fires a Bren gun.

catch in front of the magazine. This catch rotated to unlock the barrel. The gun's carrying handle was then used to remove the hot barrel without burning your hands. Later versions of the Bren gun were fitted with a chrome-lined barrel, so no spares were required.

The gun sights were mounted on the left side of the weapon because of the top-loading magazine. This meant the gun could only be fired on the right side of the body. The gunner fired from a prone position, with the weapon mounted on a bipod, or from a standing position using a tripod when the gun was used as anti-aircraft artillery. Using a sling to carry it, the Bren gun could be fired on the move or from a kneeling position in a tactical advance.

In a section of ten men, each soldier carried two spare magazines in their 1937 issue ammunition pouches for the Bren gun. Both UN forces and the enemy used the Bren gun during the Korean War. The enemy Bren guns had been supplied to the Chinese Nationalist Kuomintang forces by the British to fight the Japanese occupation during the Second World War. The communists in the subsequent Chinese Civil War had then captured the Bren guns and converted them to fire Mauser and Soviet-made ammunition. This meant an enemy Bren gun that had been made in a British factory could shoot a British soldier. The Bren gun's forbear, the Czechoslovak ZB VZ, was also widely used among the Chinese and North Korean forces because Czechoslovakia was part of the Soviet Union.

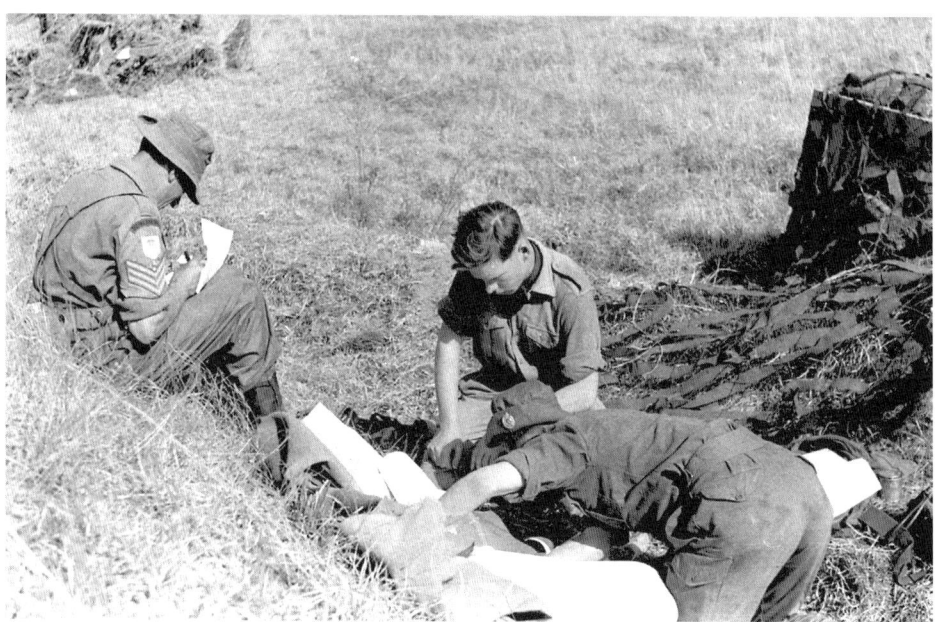

The updating of charts and filling in of reports seemed endless as light machine guns clattered, rifles cracked and helicopter rotor blades thumped the air.

Another aspect of army life was the operational briefing and waiting for the movement order. Frank said, 'We were told to be ready to move by this hour and then that hour was gone, and we were still waiting.'

'We'd be laughing and joking one minute and be a sourpuss the next. Then someone would moan about a comical misadventure, and we'd all be laughing again.'

One of Frank's comrades never went anywhere without his guitar and the music raised morale. The Royal Engineers March was called Wings and another song was called Hurrah for the CRE. The lyrics were printed in the back of The Corps of Royal Engineers history pamphlet published in 1950. Frank wasn't keen on music, but even he knew the words to It's a Long Way to Tipperary. It was a music hall favourite of the First World War that had been hated by many of the soldiers of the time. Yet, in Korea, Frank sang it with his comrades.

Inside the QLR signals truck, the operators listened to a babble of conflicting voices as messages were dispatched to and received from units in the field, as well as HQ.

The Slidex radiotelephone (R/T) code system was used during the Second World War and Korean War for sending operational messages. The code cards and three sets of card slide rulers were kept in a black wallet, which when folded measured 24.5cm by 15.7cm. When the wallet was opened for use, the width doubled to 49cm. After the Second World War, the wallet had a back panel made of 2.5mm-thick brown Pertinax flame-retardant, resin-bonded paper. The cardholder was aluminium to prevent corrosion, as was the slide ruler frames at the top and to the left of the card. On each card was printed a twelve by seventeen table of 204 rectangular word boxes. A word was printed in black ink and a single letter or number was printed in red ink in a box. At the start of the day, pairs of letters and a number were written into each cell of the horizontal and vertical sliding card rulers with a pencil. There were three sets of

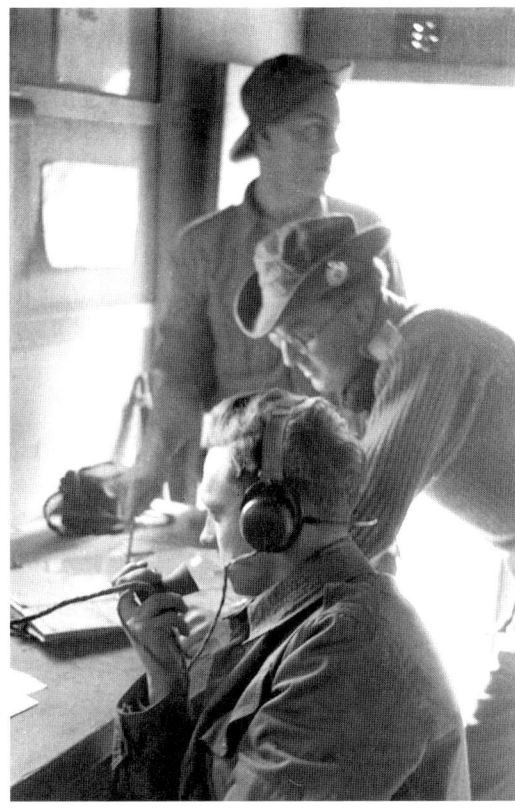

With pencils and notepads at the ready, the troop officer and wireless operators used the open Slidex code wallet on the desk to decode the messages received.

rulers. A red pencil was used for the army headquarters set, black pencil for the division HQ set and green pencil for other units. The horizontal ruler had sixteen cells and the vertical ruler twenty-one cells, both four more cells than the actual columns and rows on the code cards. This was so each ruler had five starting positions, therefore, creating the cipher key.

A Slidex message began with a three-digit code. The first number was for the decoding card that was to be used. The cards were stored in a pocket on the left side of the wallet. The second number in the message related to the cell on the horizontal ruler. The ruler was slid to the left or right to align the cell number with the top of the first column on the code card. The third number of the message was for the cell on the vertical ruler. The ruler was moved up or down to align the cell with the first row. A coded word was then transmitted as two letters. Each one matched a letter written in a cell on the horizontal and vertical rulers. The letters cross-referenced the row and column to find the word box printed on the card.

On the card was a box with 'Switch On' in red letters. When a word was not on the card, the letter code for 'Switch On' was sent. The word was spelt out as it was decoded, using the single, red-ink letters in the boxes on the card. The box 'Switch Off' was for when the spelling was complete. Numbers, such as a time, were transmitted using the same method.

In Korea, the troop officer and operators quickly and accurately decoded messages, unaware that the Slidex code had already been broken by Germany in 1944 during the Second World War. After the war, East Germany, as part of the Soviet Union, developed a similar code system and it was possible they had passed the British Slidex codes to China and North Korea.

The captain's map was of the 1st Commonwealth Division area. The thick lines were coloured red and marked the arterial road network around Kamak-san and the Gloucester Valley. These were routes 11A, 11B and Route 5Y. The minefields were meticulously recorded with a map legend explaining the type of mines and if they were buried or tripwired. The River Imjin was naturally marked in blue.

'Scheme 3' 87

The troop officer worked on huge map boards outside the signals truck under the camouflage netting. The boards depicted the terrain and reported unit positions that were marked as crossed or dotted boxes.

The captains studied the current situation.

Left: *Bread as hard as a brick with cheese made for a doorstop sandwich. It was washed down with a cup of tea in a much-needed break during operations.*

Below: *An Auster Air Observation Plane Mk 6 flew over the sappers' manoeuvres. By creating a white on black photographic negative, the serial number on its wings is revealed as 'WJ357'. Tracing this serial number revealed it was one of thirty-six aircraft manufactured between June 1952 and March 1953 by the British company of Auster Aircraft Ltd. It was delivered to the Royal Air Force. The Auster AOP 6 was a two-seat aircraft, 23-feet long and with a wingspan of 36 feet. A De Havilland Gipsy Major 7 four-cylinder, air-cooled inverted in-line piston engine powered it. The plane's maximum speed was 124 miles per hour, its range 315 miles and its operational ceiling was a height of 14,000 feet.*

In Korea, army officers of the Royal Artillery with pilots of 1903 Independent Air Observation Post Flight RAF flew Auster AOPs from the Fort George Airstrip on the Imjin. In three-hour shifts, they maintained a constant surveillance of the fortified hills of the frontline, reporting the coordinates of spotted enemy positions and movement. These targets were then destroyed by artillery barrage directed onto them by the flight crews. The first flight started an hour before sunrise. In the last sortie of the day, the crew looked for where the enemy troops were massing before a night attack upon a particular section of the battlefront. It provided early warning of, as Frank put it, 'A visit from our neighbours.'

Air observers plotted the location of forests. Frank said, 'Chinese and North Korean infantry camouflaged themselves with cut tree branches. One flight saw a forest in one location, and on the next flight, the forest was found to have magically uprooted itself and marched a noticeable distance.'

Right: *The truck was loaded with jerry cans of spare fuel ready for a move.*

Below: *The sappers were caught in a traffic jam along a narrow forest road when a Morris 15cwt truck had become stuck in a drainage ditch. The approaching traffic controller wasn't happy. Generally, some roads in the system were one-way only, but roads could be closed due to accident, for repairs after bad weather or because of enemy artillery fire.*

An officer being driven to a destination was trained to take an interest in his surroundings, making notes and marking up his map. He was then able to refer back to what he had seen along the route and pass on information about where essential engineering work was needed.

In the office truck, a sergeant is checking a sapper's 'Qualification and Record Card' (service record). The sergeant's fountain pen is hovering over the section with the 'run out' box in which the date for a sapper's service to end was always marked in pencil. The surrounding boxes would be filled in with pen if adding a voluntary service extension date.

The troop sergeant relaxes with a smoke. A good day for the surrogate father of sixty-four men plus officers and attached KSC labourers, all with an average age of 20, was when they all came back to camp alive.

Chapter 9

Stalemate

In 1945, during the Second World War, Kono Kiyoshi had been serving with the Imperial Japanese Army in Manchuria when the Russians had captured him. He had been sent to a Siberian gulag, where in May 1949 he voluntarily informed on fellow prisoners. Kono went on to become a highly trained communist agent with no national affiliation to Korea.

On 19 July 1953, Kono, then aged 31, having infiltrated through the frontline, was spotted swimming across the River Imjin by a US marine MP. This was reported in the Monthly Security Intelligence Report for July 1953.

Additional intelligence reports issued on 20 July and 23 July stated a North Korean was captured after infiltrating the 29th Infantry Brigade sector. His mission had been to sabotage military installations, but UN forces had expected the four other members of the NKPA 'Stay Behind' guerrilla unit to raid cookhouses and stores for food. A body was later found on an island inlet between the Imjin and Samichon rivers.

On 27 July 1953, the armistice was declared. However, South Korean President Syngman Rhee refused to sign, meaning a peace treaty was never reached (a state of emergency still exists today). North Korea and China, with America representing UN forces, had signed the armistice and implemented a ceasefire. After three years of war, the political position in divided Korea was now reversed. The communist north had originally invaded the south in 1950. Following its liberation, the south, aided by the UN forces, had then invaded the north. With Chinese support, North Korea had been recaptured, and its forces had begun to attack South Korea for a second time. President Rhee would not sign the armistice as he believed only a second invasion of the north by UN forces would achieve his aims of unification and victory. However, the PLA and NKPA had tunnelled into and entrenched every ridge for several miles into North Korea. Tunnels led out to ambush points at the foot of each ridge to attack any UN-led invasion force from behind.

As agreed in the armistice signed by the US and Chinese, a demilitarized zone (DMZ) was created to separate the hostile nations. All military forces withdrew from this zone taking with them all equipment, stores and munitions. Operation Swan Lake was the codename for the UN withdrawal. On 28 July 1953, 55 Field

Squadron commenced the operation by being the first to return back to the Kansas Line on the River Imjin.

On 4 August 1953, 1st Commonwealth Division Operation Instruction No. 79 'Security of Present Area' was issued. It stated, 'Enemy agents may continue to enter the divisional area. Whilst banditry may start in order to secure arms, stores, clothing and food etc.' Standing orders were issued to seal off the divisional area north and south of the River Imjin. Road checkpoints, hill and night patrols, and bridge guards were to be increased. Approaches to known fords across shallow points of the River Imjin were closed off with wire. Foot patrols were established to prevent further infiltration, such as the ones that had occurred the previous month.

On 20 August 1953, the first draft of Operation Continue was issued. If the armistice was broken by another invasion of the south, the 1st Commonwealth Division were to make a fighting withdrawal to the south bank of the River Imjin. The Royal Engineers were to provide both a ferry and M2 assault boats should the bridges be damaged in the fighting. An M2 assault boat was a plywood rowing boat that required three engineers to operate it and was able to carry an infantry squad. The sappers were to destroy the bridges when the withdrawal was complete and evacuate the bridge guard by these boats.

Frank said, 'Although an armistice was agreed and may exist on paper, it was never truly signed as hostilities continued.'

On 22 August 1953, the Royal Engineers diary stated, 'In order to decide on certain basic types of defence for the KANSAS Line, 55 Field Squadron held a demonstration in which they exhibited prefabricated MMG bunkers and gunner observation posts. Company commanders were invited to inspect and comment on the designs from a user point of view. The General in Overall Command (GOC) of the 1st Commonwealth Division and senior officers finally saw the exhibits. A decision was made on which patterns to be adopted.'

Construction work on strengthening the fortifications of the Kansas Line was underway when, on 6 September, search parties from both sides returned to the DMZ. This was to recover bodies as agreed in the armistice. The 1st Commonwealth Division named the recovery operation 'Finder'. The search parties remained strictly on their respective side of the DMZ and did not cross the demarcation line. They did not carry weapons into the DMZ, and everyone carried their ID papers. The 12 Field Squadron ensured the UN-laid minefields were clearly marked, while 64 Field Park Squadron provided dogs trained to find bodies and 55 Field Squadron assisted in the search.

Frank found a skull lying face up and was so shocked that without thinking he took a photograph of it with his Box Brownie. The photograph remained as an unprinted negative to respect the dignity of the fallen and is not included here.

When a body or part of a body was found, personal effects, equipment or tattered strips of clothing were not removed as this was the only way to identify the nationality of the remains. Only weapons were removed and made safe. A strict forensic procedure was followed to record where the body was discovered

Frank was posted to the timber camp near Tockchong jointly run by Royal Engineers and the Royal Canadian Engineers. There, the sappers accumulated engineering equipment from portable sawmills to tractors. At this camp, the sappers manufactured prefabricated bunker frames and initially shipped them to the Kansas Line along the new roads constructed by 12 Field Squadron. However, the weight of the frames and mountainous terrain made it a difficult journey that involved laborious manhandling when the road ran out. In the first week of October 1953, a solution was found, which was to use Sikorsky H-19 Chickasaw helicopters from the 1st US Marine Division to airlift the thirty frames manufactured per day directly to the construction sites. There, the frames were quickly assembled into bunkers, in pits that were 20-feet deep and had been dug by 64 Field Park Squadron and infantry regiments. Previously, a standard bunker on the Hook had been buried to 13 feet with a 5-feet-thick ceiling of concrete and earth. This earlier design had been able to withstand up to two hits from 155mm Chinese artillery.

and report if anything was found in the immediate area. Other than weapons, any items were put into a sandbag. This was tagged and placed in the casualty bag with the body. Enemy bodies were taken to a shallow temporary burial ground in the DMZ. Frank and his comrades ensured the fallen were given the utmost care, dignity and respect when buried. The graves were marked with stakes with two feet of white tape tied around them. This was so the burial ground could be clearly identified. The location was recorded on the recovery reports sent to the joint observer team. They arranged for both sides to cross the demarcation line, at an appointed time, to repatriate the dead from the burial grounds.

Operation Finder ended on 12 September 1953. Intelligence Summary No. 340 reported that the bodies of twenty-nine Chinese communist were repatriated. There was no mention of UN dead being repatriated.

The Hook had been a hill, which had been a key geological and strategic feature. It had been the gateway to the Samichon Valley and the main route into South Korea since Genghis Khan invaded in the twelfth century. The Royal Engineers, with other Commonwealth units, had fought to keep control of the Hook right up until the armistice. The hill had been extensively tunnelled to turn it into an impregnable fortress. As agreed in the armistice, the old frontline in the DMZ was 'dismantled'. The 12 Field Squadron lined the tunnels inside the Hook with explosives. On 11 September 1953, the Hook was imploded, releasing 'a charnel house stench' of unfound bodies that were still on and inside the hill as it collapsed in on itself.

The Royal Engineers' diary entry on 31 October stated, 'The regimental working party constructed 180 bunkers during the week.' The target was sixty a week. On 2 November, 'The GOC ordered a complete reconnaissance of the Imjin to discover all possible fords.' According to War Office records, a revised draft of Operation Continue was issued on 5 November. The force covering the withdrawal was expected 'to impose a four-hour delay on the enemy north of the Imjin'.

UN forces fortified the hills of the Kansas Line against an anticipated third communist invasion. Cut and cover trenches were dug as they had proved effective in the past. These were 2-feet wide, 6-feet high and roofed with concrete lintels that supported 2 feet of earth-fill, which was topped with a layer of rocks that formed a slope above. Bunkers were also covered with this layer as it dispersed the ballistic energy of a shell explosion away from structure, ensuring it and its occupants survived the blast.

The necklace-shaped trench pattern around a hill and the First World War-style zigzag communication trench and tunnel design were abandoned. Stretcher parties had found it difficult to move a patient around the blind corners. Instead, junction chambers were installed in the new fortification design. It was like two overlapping spider webs that ran through and across a hill. This ensured a more efficient removal of casualties, as well as the movement of ammunition, etc., to the most forward positions. The design mirrored that of the Chinese and North Korean fortifications.

Chapter 10

Tockchong

Frank titled the negative album 'Life and landscape in Tockchong area'. Tockchong, also known as Tokchong, is a town that had a rail terminus for troop trains. It was a base for several Commonwealth regiments and included workshops for the Royal Engineers as well as the Royal Electrical and Mechanical Engineers. Frank explored the area when he was stationed there in the late summer of 1953.

The A-frame boy matched the typical A-frame man in strength by carrying a load just as heavy, which was three times the size of a man. At any moment, it seemed the boy would collapse onto the road and be buried underneath the haystack he was carrying.

Tockchong 97

Right: *Frank called this photograph, 'Woman With Bundle'. From his shadow, which is caught in shot, he was wearing a cloth cap at the time and using a 35mm camera.*

Below: *Frank called this photograph, 'Villagers And Children', and again his shadow was caught in the picture.*

Left: *Frank titled this photograph, 'Man With Pipe'. The influx of UN soldiers to defend South Korea had caused the mass import of cigarettes from across the world. This had a detrimental effect on Korean tobacco farmers.*

Below: *In the blacksmiths, a great fog of steam and smoke glowed red as the smelting oven was stoked and the huge bellows pumped. Hot, soft metal hissed as it cooled in water buckets before being shaped on the anvil with a hammer.*

Tockchong 99

Shoppers browsed the stalls lining this street.

The children pushed and pulled the wagon along the narrow track between the paddy fields towards another area of the town.

The drainage ditch and part of the road had collapsed to become a flooded rut. A Scammell Pioneer 6×4 tractor and trailer, and the following Willy's jeep, avoided the danger because out of sight, around the corner, was a warning sign.

This street looks mainly residential.

A type-2 cattle fence was made of four coils of concertina wire laid in two rows, with each row consisting of one concertina laid on top of the other. They were fixed in place by three strands of barbed wire that had been strung across the stakes to form a 'cattle' fence. The metal stakes were 6 feet in height and driven into the ground to a depth of 18 inches and were spaced 10 feet apart. The fence was a very effective barrier.

The stalls in the market were set up in outbuildings and loaded wagons stood stationary in this market square. A type-2 cattle barbed-wire fence, the same type as used on the frontline, enclosed the market. Civilians were relatively safe from guerrilla attack while they purchased locally sourced tools, clothing and food. They also browsed the goods that Frank called 'bits and bobs' that had been acquired by travelling merchants.

From his camp, Frank photographed this pedestrian walking along the road to Tockchong's thriving market (in the background of the picture).

Chapter 11

Seoul

In Frank's archive, there were two negative albums and several slides that documented his many trips to Seoul, the South Korean capital. The sappers were repeatedly deployed there to resolve the infrastructure problems of the battle-damaged city. Frank photographed the historical landmarks as he had an interest in architecture.

In 1911, having occupied Korea for six years, Imperial Japan had started planning the construction of the Government-General Building. The German architect Georg de Lalande, who had lived in Japan since 1901, designed it. After de Lalande had died in 1914, the Japanese architect Nomura Ichiro had taken over the project. Construction had begun on 25 June 1916, starting with the demolition of the Korean palaces built by the ancient kings of the Joseon Dynasty. Japanese

The Seoul Capitol Building.

After North Korea's invasion of the south in 1950, the Capitol Building had been used as the HQ of the NKPA. Before their retreat, they had set the building ablaze, completely destroying the interior and leaving it a gutted shell. When Frank took this photograph, the grey granite walls still bore the scorch marks from the flames that had lashed up the outside of the building. President Rhee refused to have the building repaired, believing it symbolized occupation by first the Japanese, then the Americans and then North Korean military forces. (It was demolished in 1995.)

Behind the Capitol Building, a barricade of police jeeps ringed one of the royal palaces as a South Korean policeman upturned his rifle to control the excited crowd. They were anticipating the arrival of what Frank called 'VIPs'. Frank said, 'I was caught up in the crowd and couldn't get out of it.'

academic Muneyoshi Yanagi had successfully campaigned for the rest of the palaces to be saved. The Government-General Building was completed on 1 October 1926 and obscured the fourteenth-century Gyeongbokgung Palace from public view.

Japan's occupation of Korea ended in 1945 with the end of the Second World War. Under the United States Army Military Government Korea, the Government-General Building became known as the Seoul Capitol Building. On 31 May 1948, the building housed South Korea's Assembly, and on 24 July, Syngman Rhee had been sworn in as the country's first president.

Above: *Plainclothes ROK security agents watched and managed the crowd.*

Left: *Security agents objected to the presence of the army chaplain. Frank was 'encouraged' to stay by the agents because of his Box Brownie and 35mm cameras. Possibly, they thought he was officially sanctioned press.*

Seoul 105

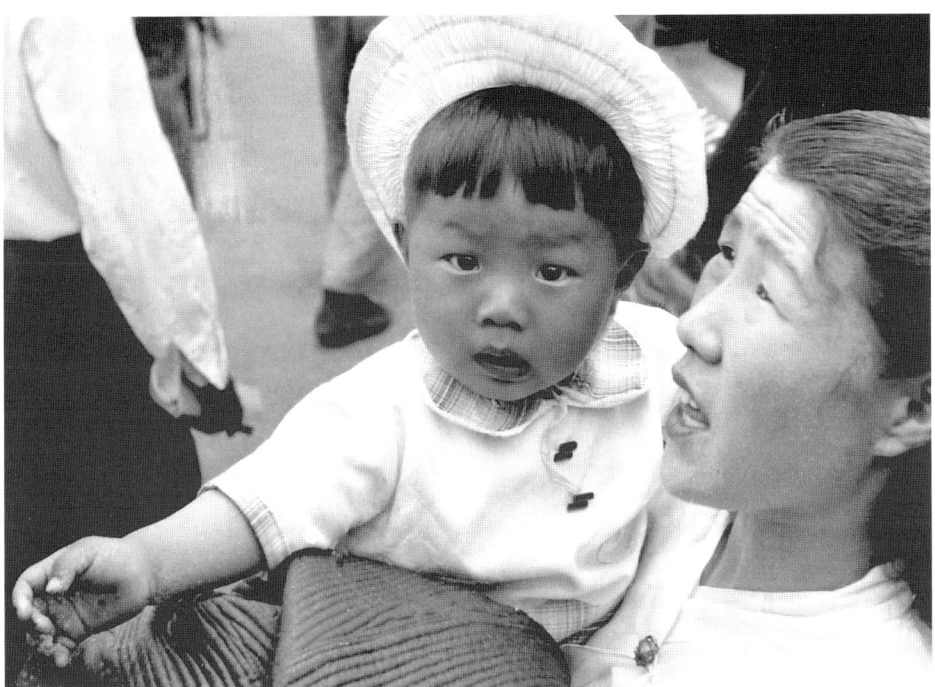

Frank's cameras fascinated this boy, who seemed oblivious to the frenetic buzz around him.

Observed by the security agents, the crowd patriotically cheered as the ROKA parade marched by with rifles braced against their shoulders. It seemed to Frank that ROKA only wanted the most muscular and tallest soldiers to show to the world, to deter North Korea from a future attack on the south.

Left: *The crowd began to disperse, with this elderly gentleman happy to pose for Frank, as the schoolboys (in their blue caps) returned to their studies.*

Below: *This group of children had gathered outside the closed Daehanmun Gate of the Deoksugung Palace to watch the parade. They now waited for permission to leave from the government agents.*

Frank visited the Changdeokgung Palace, which translates as the 'Palace of Prospering Virtue'. It had been burnt down numerous times during Korea's ancient wars and reconstructed to its original form by the ruling monarch of the time.

UN soldiers marvelled at the lotus pond in the palace grounds.

The palace gardens contained various trees and plants that formed a sculptured landscape in which the buildings complemented the tranquil setting.

Frank was allowed to enter the palace to photograph the throne room. This is how it looked in 1953. The palace was the final residence of Korea's last emperor, Sunjong, who died in 1926.

Frank visited the Sungnyemun, meaning 'Honouring Propriety Gate'. This was the official name for it as decreed by the South Korean government. King Taejo had the original gate constructed from stone and timber from 1395 to 1398. The gate had been the only place where diplomats were allowed to pass through the city's 20-feet-high fortress wall. It was one of eight gates placed in the wall. The Joseon Dynasty chronicles suggest the gates were named after the directions in which they stood, so this was the Great South Gate. The Korean word for 'Great South Gate' was later associated with the cruelty inflicted upon the people during Japan's occupation. To speak this word became an offensive slur.

During the Japanese occupation, when the Crown Prince of Imperial Japan had visited Seoul, he was believed by the Japanese to be too high-ranking to pass through the gate. The people were forced to destroy the wall around it to allow him to enter the city. The rest of the city wall was later pulled down to make way for the Japanese-imposed traffic system.

In 1907, when the streetcar network was expanded, the Sungnyemun Gate had been permanently closed. In 1938, the Japanese Governor-General had declared the gate to be the first national treasure of Korea. In the Korean War, it suffered extensive damage in the many battles for Seoul.

The Japanese architect Tatsuno Kingo had designed the Bank of Korea (shown in photograph at bottom of next page) in 1907. Opposite the bank is the stump of a building with wooden panel scaffolding mounted upon it. This was because the entire upper floors had been destroyed in the same air raid that had burned the Bank of Korea.

During the drought of 1899, American imported streetcars had arrived in Seoul. To the people, it was a metal monster, whose electrical cables disturbed the rain spirits and tracks disrupted the sleep of the Great Dragon who lived beneath the city. After an accident in which a child was killed by having been hit by a streetcar, two of them were burned in rioting. The rioters had then threatened to destroy the system's power station as its construction was said to have defiled consecrated land. The streetcar service was suspended for two weeks while order was restored and during that time it rained, confirming the people's beliefs.

A few streetcars survived and were still running through the ruined city. This one is passing the fire-blackened shell of the Bank of Korea, with its imposing, castle-like peaked corner tower.

The streetcar stopped outside the PX (Post Exchange). The PX was the American version of the British NAAFI, only on a huge, department store scale and staffed by Korean women. American soldiers were known to visit it straight from the frontline, still wearing helmets and combat fatigues, and carrying their weapons. They purchased a wide range of confectionary, tobacco and soft drinks or a six-pack of beer from the shelves. At Christmas, they browsed the sample of electrical products displayed in glass cabinets. A soldier was able to arrange for a toaster to be shipped from an American warehouse to his home in the US as a present for his family. The PX didn't take the British armed forces pound currency known as 'BAFF' notes that the Commonwealth soldiers were paid in. This created a thriving and very profitable unlawful currency exchange with American soldiers, in which the BAFF notes could be swapped for US dollars.

Due to a shortage of fuel, some cars were gas powered. The cars all looked identical and as if they had rolled straight out of a factory. Imports from the American automobile industry were a significant presence in 1953. However, some cars were Soviet copies imported from China and North Korea, and Frank found it very hard to tell them apart.

The Chosen Government Railway operated the station until 1945, when the Korean National Railroad (KNR) was established. In August 1950, a month into

The smart paintwork of the Korean buses covered the fact the parts were cobbled together from cannibalized civilian and military vehicle wreckage. Engines coughed, radiators hissed and gears clanked into place. Uneven suspension made for a rickety ride and misaligned wheels and weak tyres caused a wonky shopping trolley effect.

Seoul Railway Station was originally named Keijo Station. It was designed by Tsukamoto Yasushi of Tokyo Imperial University and was finished in November 1925. It was a red brick building with a Byzantine-type central dome. The central hall had granite paving slabs on its ground floor, and the internal walls were bare stone. The VIP lounge had birch-wood walls and a wooden floor, and the station's second floor had a restaurant with westernized decor.

Seoul Anglican Cathedral, as photographed by Frank in 1953, with its original white roof tiles.

the war, the South Korean part of the KNR was taken over and run by US Army 3rd Transportation Military Railway Service. During the battle of Seoul, the NKPA had dug trenches around the railway station. After the liberation, these positions were filled in and grassed over. A UN forward marshalling area was set up near the station as the military still made extensive use of the railway.

In 1889, Charles John Corfe became the first bishop of the Anglican Church of Korea. Construction of the Seoul Anglican Cathedral began in 1922 and was completed in 1926. Its official name is the Cathedral Church of Saint Mary the Virgin and Saint Nicholas.

Born in 1882, Alfred Cooper had been ordained into the Anglican priesthood in England in 1907. The following year, he had become a missionary priest in Korea. He then returned to England, where in 1931 at St Paul's Cathedral he was consecrated as the fourth bishop in Korea. In 1945, following the Japanese surrender at the end of the Second World War, he had returned to Korea. In 1950, he had been captured by the NKPA. Alongside 700 American soldiers and sixty-eight civilians, including the elderly and children, he had been forced, himself in his late

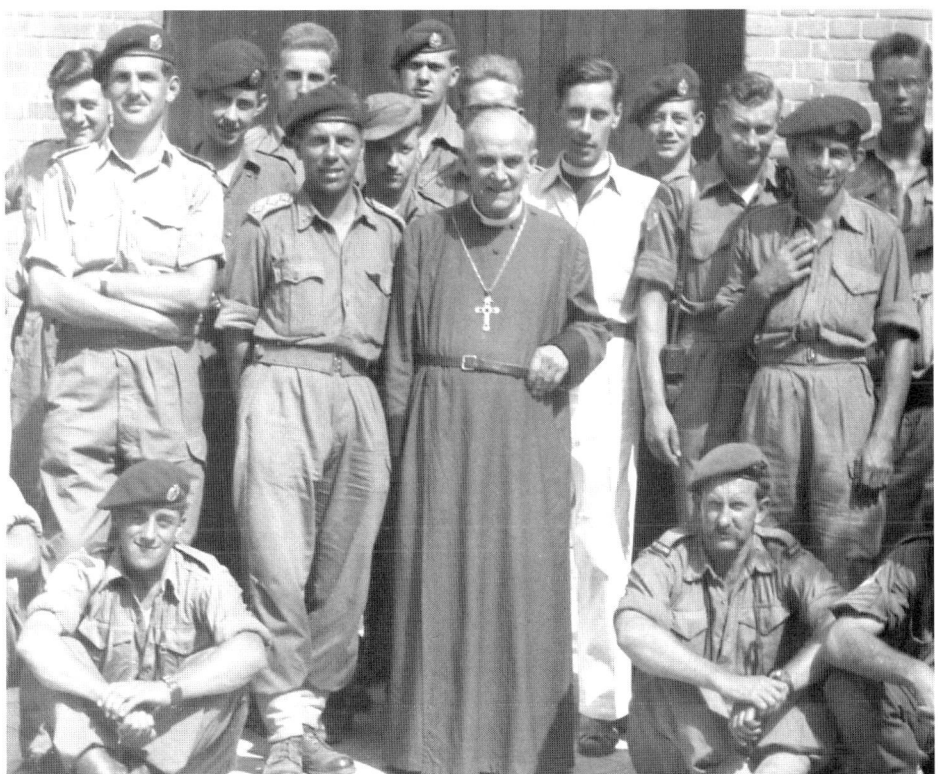

Bishop Alfred Cecil Cooper with a congregation of servicemen, circa 1953.

sixties, on a death march to a POW camp on the Chinese North Korean border of the Yalu River. It had taken nine days to march between 100 and 150 miles, of which the bishop had recalled, 'The longest distance we marched in any one day on this terrible journey was 15 miles.'

The only food the prisoners had been given was a dry ball of millet in the morning and another in the evening. The death toll is unknown, but it was estimated that at least ninety-six prisoners died during the march. Among them was Sister Mary-Clare. Born Clare Emma Whitty on 30 May 1883, she had died on 6 November 1950. The elderly Father Charles Hunt had been dragged along when he could no longer walk and had also died.

In a House of Commons debate on 11 December 1950, the Secretary of State for Foreign Affairs had been asked about the missing clergy, 'and what steps are being taken to secure their release'. In the first winter of captivity, the prisoners were only issued with adequate clothing to survive the extreme cold when China had taken over the running of the prison camps.

The bishop was released and repatriated to Britain in 1953 and on 23 April spoke of his experience at a press conference in London. He then returned to Korea, arriving in Pusan on 6 November 1953 and travelled on to Seoul. That is where Frank met and photographed him.

Here Frank discovered a moment that for him symbolized life and death. A man waits on the threshold of a place of worship, speaking to the elderly gatekeeper or caretaker. In sermons, Frank had often heard, 'One day, we shall stand at the heavenly gates.'

Chapter 12

Tokyo

On the Kansas Line, Frank took a dawn walk along a fog-shrouded jeep track.

Korea was known as the 'Land of Morning Calm' because at daybreak there was rarely a sound as the morning fog dissolved away.

Tokyo 117

A sapper burns the previous night's corned-beef tins on a rubbish fire.

At the Royal Engineer quarry, KSC labourers lined a cliff face with explosive cord to under-mine it. The several tons of rock already mined had not provided enough hardcore to fill in the newly formed potholes, which had been caused by the previous night's frost damage to the roads.

Frank and the workers took cover before detonation.

120   The Royal Engineers in Korea: The Photographic Memoir of Frank Merritt

Frank said, 'In demolition, less is more. You use a small amount of explosive that you think won't be enough to do the job. After the explosion, the pressure of a structure's own weight collapses it.'

The explosion cut deep into the stone and the entire rock face collapsed into a fall that generated a fog of dust. Frank was excused road repair duty as he had accumulated enough time in Korea to earn rest and recuperation leave. He was sent to Kimpo Airfield in Seoul to catch a flight to Tokyo, Japan.

The United States Military Air Transport Service (MATS) had begun operating on 1 June 1948 and had taken over strategic airlift operations from the US Air Force and US Navy. It was commanded by the Secretary of Defence with its operations chief appointed from the air force or navy.

MATS had played a crucial role in the Berlin Airlift using various types of aircraft including the Lockheed 749 Constellation C-121A. Once that campaign was successfully completed, the plane was converted from ferrying cargo to passengers by installing windows into its fuselage and adding removable seating. The plane could transport up to forty-five passengers or, when used for medical evacuation flights, twenty stretchers and medical staff.

The nose of the C-121A was converted to a distinctive shape, and it was the first American aircraft to be fitted with all-weather radar. The plane also had a distinctive triple tail, and in Korea, plane '8609' in the photograph, had a white chassis with chrome silver wings and belly. It had a crew of six to eight, who were

A Lockheed 749 Constellation C-121A.

pilot, co-pilot, radio operator, engineer and two to four flight attendants. It was 95-feet long with a wingspan of 123 feet and was 23-feet high. It was powered by four 2200hp Wright R-3350-75 eighteen-cylinder, air-cooled radial piston engines with three bladed propellers. Its speed was 330 miles per hour, it had an operational ceiling of 25,000 feet and a range of 2400 miles.

Frank was looking forward to sitting in a seat and being catered for by a flight attendant as he flew to Tokyo. There was just a minor problem: Frank was booked on the wrong plane for that.

Frank's flight to Japan was on the colossal monster of the sky that was a Douglas C-124 Globemaster II. It was a heavy-lift cargo transport, 130-feet long, with a wingspan of 174 feet and it was 48-feet high. It had a crew of seven, who were the aircraft commander, pilot, navigator, flight engineer, radio operator and two loadmasters. Its maximum speed was 304 miles per hour and its operational ceiling was 21,800 feet. Its range depended on the combined weight of its cargo, fuel and the actual plane itself. At its maximum weight, it was able to travel for 1000 miles.

The plane had two large clamshell doors and a hydraulic ramp in the nose, plus a cargo elevator under the aft fuselage. Its 77-feet-long cargo bay had a storage capacity of 10,000 cubic feet and was fitted with two overhead hoists, which were individually capable of lifting 8000lb (3600kg). The maximum load it could carry

A Douglas C-124 Globemaster II.

was 68,500lb (31,100kg). This could be anything from military hardware, such as tanks, guns and trucks, to the heavy construction machinery the Royal Engineers used. In a passenger-carrying role, it was able to transport 200 fully equipped troops on its double decks. When acting as an air ambulance, it could transport 127 patients with nursing staff.

The aircraft was powered by four large Pratt & Whitney R-4360 Wasp Major twenty-eight-cylinder, air-cooled radial piston engines. Each engine, with its water-cooling and alcohol fuel-injection system, generated 3800hp. Frank marvelled at the spin of the Curtis C634S three-blade propellers, each 16 feet in diameter.

'Old Shaky', as the plane was known, was living up to its name. The sergeant asked, 'First time in a plane, Frank?' Frank replied, 'Apparently the officers' plane has seats.'

The Douglas Aircraft Company in Long Beach, California, manufactured the Globemaster. The innovation for the plane came after the Berlin Airlift of 1948. That operation had created the necessity for a heavy lift giant of the air.

A British Commonwealth forces bus took Frank and his comrades from the airport to Ebisu Camp in a Tokyo suburb. As soon as a soldier on leave signed in at reception, his leave officially started. The officers took a taxi to a hotel. For the men at the camp, then came their first hot shower in months. The soldiers were then issued with a clean, pressed uniform. They were shown to the dining hall, where they could have a meal at a table, which was served to them by the 'angels' of the Women's Voluntary Service. Frank said 'Some soldiers studied the cutlery before eating as if they had never seen a knife and fork before. It was a sign they had spent considerable time on the battlefield.'

Afterwards, Frank and his comrades were allocated a room with an actual bed with clean, white sheets. The soldiers were told the beds would be made up for them every day. Frank said, 'I was beginning to realize why the sergeant called rest and recuperation leave the rack and ruin of a soldier because we were spoiled with luxury. It was get up when you want, have a shower and have breakfast, with no one shooting at you.'

Frank wrote, 'On arrival in Tokyo on Sunday the 3rd January 1954, I had a little time left to go into Tokyo itself where I brought the book 'Japan The Pocket Guide' with this and tours by the W.V.S. [Women's Volunteer Service] I was able to see and photograph as much as possible on Tokyo also a little of Kamakure and Yokohama.'

Frank purchased an aquamarine, hardback notebook with a blue taped spine. On the cover he wrote, 'holiday notes'. He felt confident enough to battle his dyslexia and write about his time in Tokyo.

'Monday the 4th of January 1954 I had a general look at Ebisu, which is a suburb of Tokyo, where the rest centre was. In the afternoon I went on a tour where I saw the Memorial Picture Gallery to the Emperor, which showed the life of the Emperor and the change, which took place at the time in Japan, after three

'In that evening I obtained a night picture of Ginza the main shopping centre of Tokyo.'

'The Yasukuni Shrine is a memorial to all those who lost their lives in the wars.'

hundred years of military rule. From there it was onto the Yasukuni Shrine passing the Akasaka palace, which was originally home of the Emperor before he moved to the Imperial Palace.'

Above: *'Tuesday the 5th of January 1954 I visited the Meji Shrine, which is dedicated to the Emperor Meji and then went by the Imperial Palace gardens where I saw a few old Japanese buildings but not the palace.'*

Right: *'That afternoon I went to the Ueno Park. I saw the Toshogu Shrine and the Pagoda.'* Frank had been awarded the Queen's Korean medal and UN Korean medal and wore the ribbons on his uniform above the chest pocket.

'I also went to the Zoological Gardens.' Children were drawing pictures at this stone lamp.

Above left: *'Wednesday the 6th of January 1954 I spent the whole day in Tokyo. I walked around the Diet Building (Japanese parliament) and saw the Imperial Palace. Near there were many girls in national dress.'*

Above right: Frank captioned this photograph, *'girl with a teddy bear'*.

Right: *'I also saw a Buddhist Temple known as the Nishi-Hongan-Ji.'*

Left: *Frank called this photograph, 'boy with a kite at the temple'.*

Below: *'After this I walked down the Ginza and went in many large buildings that contain a number of shops.'*

'Thursday 7th of January 1954 I was on an all day tour to Kamakura where the Great Buddha was.' The Great Buddha is a 44-feet bronze statue forged in 1250 AD and is still a must see when visiting Japan. Kamakura was an hour and a half away by the soldiers' tour bus from Tokyo.

'I also went on Enoshima Island.'

'On the connecting footbridge spanning across the sea a woman sold shellfish.'

Stepping off the bridge into what Frank called the 'entrance to the island'. On the right of the photograph was another woman selling shellfish and straight ahead was 'the main street of Enoshima'.

Left: *'There are many souvenir shops,'* Frank recorded in his notebook.

Below: *'The island goes up many feet above sea level so there are many steps to climb. The Island is picturest [picturesque] in itself.'*

Facing out to sea was 'a cave known as the Dragon Cave'.

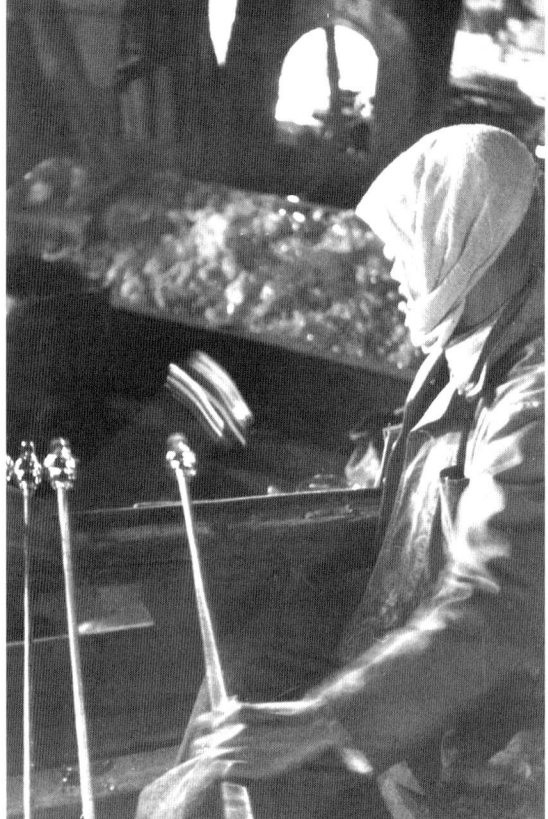

Above: *'Friday the 8th of January 1954 I had a general walk around Tokyo.'* Frank photographed this suburban home.

Left: *'In the afternoon I visited a glass and china factory. I saw the general run from the start to the finish of china making, also the painting of the china. At the glass factory I saw the glass being blown, rolled to form the shape required, making and placing a handle, glass engraving and sand blasting.'*

Above: *'Matting the glass.'*

Right: *'Engraving the glass.'*

136   The Royal Engineers in Korea: The Photographic Memoir of Frank Merritt

Above: *'After the china was blasted any rubber material was removed.'*

Left: *'Painting China.'*

Frank wrote, 'Saturday the 9th of January 1954 after a restful morning, I went on a tour to Yokohama in the afternoon where I saw the British Commonwealth war graves and the Bluff a hill over looking Yokohama harbour. On this hill is a foreign cemetery.'

Frank was interested in art. The Japanese education system was called 6334. A child spent six years in primary school, three in lower secondary, three in upper secondary and four years in college. Social and cultural studies were actively encouraged. In Britain at that time pupils left education at 14. In Japan, the leaving age was 16.

Frank went to visit the National Museum and having trained as a silversmith was disappointed. 'There was no silverware only a few pieces of bronze. In the afternoon I rested thinking about the past week.'

Above left: *'Sunday the 10th of January 1954 the dullest day for it was very misty all day so I went to Ueno Park.'*

Above right: *'Boy painting in Ueno Park.'*

Left: *'Monday morning the 11th of January 1954 I had my last look at Ebisu.'*

Below: *Frank ended his notes here, frustrated by his dyslexia. Interested in trains, he visited Ueno train station. Forty-two trains, including four express trains, ran every day to northern Japan. To the Pacific coast of Japan, twenty-six trains, including two express trains, ran every day. Electric trains connected Tokyo to its suburbs and immediate neighbouring cities.*

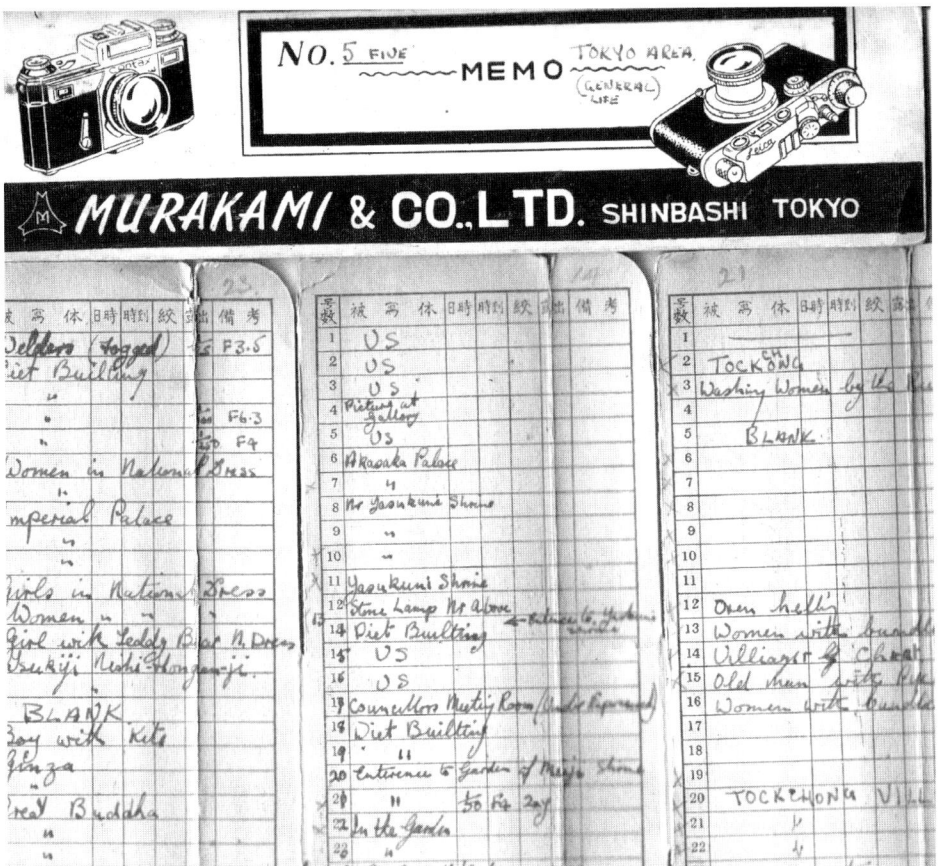

Murakami & Co Ltd negative albums. Frank visited a camera shop in Shinbashi. It was a district of Tokyo just off the Ginza. He had his films of Seoul, Tockchong and Tokyo developed there, and the negatives were placed into six cardboard jacket and tissue paper albums. Frank noted down what some of the photographs were on the lists inside the albums.

Chapter 13

Winter

'Cold, this isn't cold. You don't know what cold is, not until you've experienced a Korean winter.' Frank told me this almost every year for the rest of his life.

The 1st Commonwealth Division's 'one winter rule' was that no one should serve more than seventeen weeks of winter. The season was officially recognized as running from 1 December to 31 March. Yet, some sappers re-enlisted and endured a second winter because they believed the job they had been sent out to do wasn't finished. The 28 Field Engineer Regiment Intelligence Summary No. 47, issued in December 1953, warned that enemy agents had attempted to infiltrate the divisional area. It added that 'banditry may start in forward areas as it has done in the rear'. To counter this, checkpoints were set up and hill patrols established.

On 19 December 1953, Intelligence Summary No. 353, titled 'Enemy Intelligence Activities', reported the capture and interrogation of a North Korean agent. His name was Kim Yong Whan and he was aged 13. He had received three months' training at the Anti-South Juvenile Espionage Agents Training Centre in North Korea. This espionage school was 'training approximately 320 boys, mostly 12 to 14 years old and about 50 men and 30 women aged 17 to 25 years old'.

Having infiltrated into South Korea, Kim's mission had been to recruit youths under the age of 14 for espionage activities. The Monthly Intelligence Security Report of July 1953, titled 'Subversive Activities', had reported on the subversive training of boys by the NKPA. 'The chief subversive advantage offered by under fourteens is that no identity documents are issued or required by civilian authority.' The NKPA hoped to recruit from the thousands of orphans and vagrants roaming South Korea seeking work as civilian labour with UN forces. As winter set in, UN commanders were instructed to 'satisfy in their own mind that such agents are not presently employed in their units'.

Frank started the new year of 1954 on R&R (rest and recuperation) in Tokyo but returned on 14 January to a frozen land. Snow had packed down into ice, with the Royal Engineers having to sand dangerous spots on the roads. It seemed nature itself was fighting them in the Korean hills. It snowed again that evening, with the roads in the divisional area becoming so treacherous that traffic was cut to essential vehicles only. The continued snow and ice slowed up the MSR (main

For 55 Field Squadron, Christmas was a welcome respite of turkey and beer from the increasing workload and heavy rain as the weather deteriorated.

supply route) resurfacing programme. Some regiments used skid chains on their vehicles. These ripped up the road surface, making the situation worse.

On 15 January 1954, Intelligence Summary No 15. on 'Enemy Activity' reported that despite reduced visibility, male and female civilians had been seen close to the DMZ. This was the first sighting of civilians following a propaganda announcement of North Korea's new agricultural policy. When Frank heard of this he thought, 'they were enemy sappers because no farmer could work in that weather'.

The thick winter clothing that had been issued to the sappers in 1953 seemed adequate in the biting wind and the consistent heavy blizzard. For Frank, as the temperature dropped as low as minus thirty degrees centigrade, it seemed inconceivable that his predecessors had survived the winter of 1950 in skimpy tropical uniforms. They had been completely unprepared for this regular but extreme change in Korean weather. In January 1954, Frank witnessed spirals of barbed wire decorated with ice stalagmites. The ground was frozen solid down to a depth of six feet and it was impossible to dig through. The buckets of excavators and ram blades of bulldozers became immovable. Truck drivers and tank crews carried corrugated iron or piles of straw to park their vehicles on, to avoid them becoming frozen to the ground. When that happened, the vehicle couldn't be moved for months, until the ground had thawed. You couldn't even push it with another vehicle as the strain would burn out the engine. It couldn't be towed either because the fixings would break in the cold and the tow cable could whiplash, cutting anyone in the way in half. A vehicle was started up on the hour and the gears worked through to avoid the engine seizing up. The frost split battery casings open and bled out their chemical contents. Petrol and oil froze in fuel lines and even in the jerry cans. Hot water turned to ice in seconds when exposed to the air. The River Imjin was an Arctic-like glacier that vehicles could drive across. It allowed the NKPA infiltrators to cross too, after they had slipped through the frontline by a valley floor between the fortified hills. The NKPA offensive strategy had previously been to drip-feed its guerrillas behind the lines, assemble them into a sizeable force and then attack targets in the rear area. This could cut off the UN soldiers positioned on the frontline.

While officers from some regiments saw out the winter with ski-holidays in Japan, the sappers were working through the worst of it. Communications between units were often intermittent due to the radio signal cutting out in atrocious weather. Broken battery casings added to the problem. The sappers risked frostbite to their fingers and hands because they couldn't always work in thick gloves. Their flesh could become frozen, meaning the blood couldn't circulate and if left untreated fingers would just snap off a hand. Bare metal couldn't be touched because the cold acted like glue and it could take the skin off your hand. Frank couldn't work his camera or fire a rifle in those conditions, yet mines had to be laid to try to stop infiltration. Other mines had to be made safe and cleared before they became 'pirate' mines. If they were left, the chemical fuses in the anti-tank mines that had been laid the previous winter degraded, making them highly sensitive and too dangerous to approach. The warning signs and perimeter fencing were renewed to warn friend, foe and civilian to stay away.

Sappers fell ill with pneumonia and flu. Nagging chest ailments flared up among the older veterans who stubbornly refused to report sick. They were ordered to join the casualties being flown out to Japan.

On both sides of the DMZ, opposing forces exercised in mountain warfare. On 20 January 1954, 55 Field Squadron trained in the Royal Engineer-designed Exercise Jack Rabbit and occupied the Kansas Line positions. The sappers took on a frontline infantry role training to assist in the counter-attack of an enemy winter offensive. Intelligence reports were proved right when, despite the reduced visibility, recently shipped-in Soviet T34 tanks were spotted as China increased its forces.

The reduced speed limit for load-carrying vehicles was 15 miles per hour due to deteriorating road surfaces within the divisional area. This led to a resumption of civilians stealing from moving military vehicles. On 30 January 1954, the 4th Field Squadron of the 25th Canadian Infantry Brigade commanded the joint Operation Pole Cat 3. This was to clear out unauthorized personnel north of the River Imjin. The ramshackle shantytowns were searched for munitions, military equipment and 'suspect material'. Civilians authorized to be in the area had an employee identity card or a certificate, denoting ROKA or KSC, issued by the police. Twenty-plus people without documentation were 'evacuated' from the area. As well as 'illegal entrants' to the area, child thieves and enemy agents were captured. Military equipment was confiscated, and stolen goods were recovered. However, it was reported in the Intelligence Summary dated 1 February that an estimated 700 bandits, resembling in appearance and tactics the 'Stay Behind' NKPA guerrillas, were at large in the rear area. They sporadically engaged the ROKA upon an ice-covered battlefield. For once, Frank very wisely didn't wander out of camp, due to the weather conditions and the fighting.

On 1 February 1954, the headquarters of the Royal Engineers (HQRE) produced the first issue of the in-house magazine the *Kansas Tract Journal of The Royal Imjineers*. It only ran for a few issues. On 9 February 1954, 55 Field Squadron resurfaced Route 1X. On 10 February, 12 Field Squadron occupied the frontline positions for Exercise Jack Rabbit. In daytime, the snow was replaced by torrential rain. In the afternoon, the cold Siberian wind from the north was at its worst and the freeze continued.

The Kansas Line tents were equipped with stoves or oil drip heaters. These replaced the cobbled-together contraptions the sappers had built in previous winters that had given off toxic fumes. The stove or heater was placed in the centre of the tent on a table-like base that was 3 inches high, in a sand box, to allow cooling air to circulate and protect the wooden floor from fire. The pipe chimney ran through an insulating sleeve as it passed through the A-frame construction roof of the tent. The sleeve was large enough to create a 3-inch air space around the pipe. An 18-inch square, metal flue plate held the pipe in place, and small drill holes in the plate allowed air to flow and cool it. With the oil drip heaters, if the oil flowed too quickly, the chimney became too hot and set the tent ablaze. A fire bucket of sand was kept inside the tent, and the fuel was outside. Decanting of fuel was by means of a tap screwed into the drum to avoid spillage. That was if the fuel wasn't frozen solid. Only the fuel specified for each type of heater was used. The unit fire officer inspected any improvised stove before installation.

Heated rocks were used to warm sleeping bags. The sleeping bags quickly became dirty with grime from winter clothing, but this clothing couldn't be washed as it would destroy its waterproofing. Of a morning, a sapper would go outside to the water barrel and smash the ice into dinner-plate sized chunks for a cold shave. It was uncomfortable, but it was better to have a washed and clean-shaven face than a bushy beard hiding painful, infected cold sores. Frank said, 'To the Americans, being clean-shaven made us look smart and as if the cold didn't bother us.'

Frank huddled with his comrades in his tent to keep warm as rum was passed around. He refused it and was told, 'You might be teetotal Frank, but the one thing you can have with us, mate, is a smoke.'

Frank had his first roll-up cigarette. The minuscule heat from the burning cigarette warmed his thick, chubby fingers. Chain-smoking was to ruin his health in later life.

Chapter 14

The Road

The floodwater of the spring thaw carried an enormous landslide of boulders and grassy mire. It accumulated into a towering dam that filled a hill pass for miles. It buried the road that Frank and his comrades had battled all winter to keep open.

Above: *The roadside ditches and drainage tunnels were frozen solid with huge blocks of ice that were insulated from the warming weather by the accumulated rock spill and sludge. Bulldozers or diggers couldn't cut through it. The sappers had to manually dig down to chop out the iceberg-blocked culverts.*

Right: *In some places the only way to get rid of the blockage was to use explosives.*

146 The Royal Engineers in Korea: The Photographic Memoir of Frank Merritt

Above: *The blast turned flood debris into a pillar of powdery fallout that was carried by the wind towards the watching sappers.*

Left: *A sapper used a pneumatic drill to chisel apart more of the rocks that buried the road.*

Right: *The tops and bottoms of empty fuel barrels were cut off. These would be laid on their sides to use as new drainage tunnels for the road.*

Below: *The sappers enjoyed a well-earned sandwich and a cup of tea at a works hut.*

Left: *A sapper has a smoke before he continues road building. His cap badge bears the initials of the late King George VI.*

Below: *55 Field Squadron's KSC labourers were known as the Road Legion. In a long line, they carried out the gruelling and Herculean task of digging out the road, with water hoses creating a fine mist to suppress the dust smog.*

The sappers discuss how to clear the next blockage along the road.

The labourers heave a huge boulder away.

Above: *The boulder tumbled downhill, causing an avalanche of stone but thankfully away from the road repair.*

Left: *With the road cleared and the drainage tunnels in place, the floodwater ditches were re-dug ready for the monsoon floods that would come in July. Frank said about the KSC labourers doing the road repairs, 'As usual they worked long hours and gave it their all, just like everything else they did. You couldn't fault them.'*

With the road cleared of the mountainous dam of flood debris, the morning daily survey for overnight frost damage was carried out. It was the same procedure for all roads. The officers responsible for ensuring this road remained open walked along it. To the side was its new run-off stream.

Damage reports sent to HQ would include the severity of the damage, time it was first seen, the effect on traffic and what traffic control had been organized. This was in accordance with Operation Amazon – the monsoon flood precaution plan. With Korea's extreme weather conditions, the roads were graded with the traffic-light system of surveying, which specified what vehicles a road was capable of carrying on a particular day. When graded red due to bad weather, only heavy convoys of essential supplies to the frontline, such as munitions, would be allowed to travel. Even then, it required a vehicle pass signed by unit command. No tracked vehicles would be allowed on the road without authorization from HQ. The Royal Engineers' vehicles and ambulances were granted unrestricted travel at all times. When the roads were graded amber, it was necessary to keep traffic to a minimum. No vehicles were allowed on the roads unless in possession of a vehicle pass signed by an officer. A road left unrepaired and without these measures in place often crumbled to nothing as soon as it was driven upon.

The Centurion tank was produced in 1945 and had a crew of four that was a commander, driver, gunner and loader, who also doubled as a radio operator. The Centurion tank was 32-feet long and 11-feet wide, with a height of 9 feet. It was

Centurion tanks camouflaged with long grass and branches passed by. The tank exhausts belched fumes that carried a burning smell that mixed with earth thrown off the tracks to sting the back of the nose and throat. Seeing tanks on the move was a morale booster to the 55 Field Squadron sappers and the Road Legion. The labourers proudly wore diamond shoulder badges, yellow with black trim and 'KSC' emblazoned in black capital letters. The tanks ploughed parallel tracks into the road that then needed to be repaired. It was a minor inconvenience compared to the huge undertaking of clearing away a mountainous landslide.

able to ford the River Imjin up to a depth of 4 feet and clamber over an obstacle up to 3 feet in height. The Centurion Mark 3 was armed with a 20-pound cannon and a .303 heavy machine gun. It was powered by a Rolls-Royce Meteor 650hp engine. Its maximum speed was 22 miles per hour, with a range of 50 miles. Its armoured plating was 152mm thick on the front of the turret. A recovery vehicle and a 105mm cannon variant of the tank were also used in Korea. The Centurion tank was highly regarded by their crews, who had faced suicide attacks by enemy sappers armed with petrol bombs and spear-tipped explosives known as a pole charge. The spear was rammed between the wheels of a tank if the enemy got close enough. It was a tactic that was also being used in the Indochina War (1946–54) by the Communist People's Army of Vietnam against French forces, with a similar weapon called the Lunge Mine. This was a high-explosive anti-tank mine fixed to the end of a pole.

On hot, dry days, the ground baked, dissolving into powder. Truck wheels ploughed up the road into a choking fog of white dust. This three-ton truck had taken the bend too fast and had come off the road. Thankfully, it had toppled into a field, rather than crushing the house opposite. Frank saw many road accidents caused by speeding and referred to the drivers as 'stupid mad bastards'.

The Royal Electrical and Mechanical Engineers 1st Infantry Troops Recovery Unit drove Scammell Pioneer SV2S Heavy Breakdown Tractors.

The family from the nearby house watched the wreck be raised and slam back down onto its wheels. The cable was fixed to the front of the wreck. It was raised off its mangled front wheels to be towed back to camp.

The weather could change dramatically from one day to the next. Here, heavy rain has turned the road and surrounding countryside into a vast, porridge-like swamp.

The British company Scammell Lorries Ltd first produced this 6×4 off-road vehicle in 1927 and originally there were no plans for its military use. It was fitted with a walking beam suspension and a Gardner six-cylinder diesel engine that provided incredible towing strength over rough ground. Its three-ton extendable crane could add to this. To operate it on soft terrain, a pair of caterpillar tracks could be placed over the rear wheels to convert the tractor into a half-track vehicle.

By 1954, rescuing a three-ton truck wreck had unfortunately become routine. A cable was run from one recovery vehicle parked in front of the wreck, through the D-ring of the vehicle parked behind. The cable was then attached to the top of the wreck. The engineer, with his back to the camera, hand signalled to the front recovery vehicle as it inched slowly forward along the road.

Frank accepted a lift back to camp from a truck driver he knew. By then, he was a regular sight, out walking with his cameras.

Chapter 15

The Castle Inn

Frank wrote 'Castle Inn NAAFI being finished' with a blue fountain pen on the blue cover of a negative album he had numbered 'K2A' in pencil. Another note in pen, 'General at the Castle Inn', was written on the cream cover of a brown-lettered album from the 'Westminster Photographic Exchange Ltd, London'. The photographs were of the Royal Engineers' project to construct a convoy stopover point just behind the frontline. It was built in the style of an old English pub and looked out of place in an active war zone.

The construction of the Castle Inn NAAFI was a surprising venture being that it was at a time of rising political tension and military build-up. Commonwealth Division Intelligence Summary No. 363, which was issued on 1 March 1954, reported:

> 'North Korean Government has started training additional guerrilla forces to provide reinforcements for those presently operating in South Korea. The source stated that approx 5,000 men selected from the NKPA or the NK Volunteer corps as having battle experience or a having a good knowledge of South Korean geography are being trained in Pyongyang. The first group of trainees is allegedly scheduled to complete their training in time to enter South Korea in the early spring. Their aim is stated to be the disruption of the elections for the ROK national assembly in May 1954.'

55 Field Squadron began the construction of the Castle Inn on 8 March 1954. The site chosen was the base of an Imjin hill, landmarked by the ruins of a thirteenth-century castle that had been built after the invasion by Genghis Khan.

Lieutenant Colonel Edgar Frank Brawn of the Royal Engineers invented the Romney hut during the Second World War in answer to the shortage of material for the construction of facilities. The hut was a tubular steel frame comprising four curved segments bolted together in a semi-circular arch shape and covered in sheets of corrugated iron. Before assembly on site, the sheets could have windows and doors cut into them to adapt the hut to what it was going to be

A stone brick chimney was built for the Castle Inn's fireplace.

Above: *The timber skeleton of the inn was assembled.*

Left: *The frame for the external log beam walls was put together and hauled upright and into position by rope.*

The Castle Inn 159

Right: *Stone boundary walls were built around the grounds of the Castle Inn.*

Below: *To the left and to the rear of the Castle Inn, Romney huts have been built. To the right and in front of the inn, a bandstand and gardens were under construction.*

A Romney hut at the Castle Inn.

used for. This could range from administration, industrial or an accommodation role. The standard hut was 96-feet long and 35-feet wide. The total amount of steel used for each hut was less than ten tons. The Romney hut was used in all theatres of operations during the Second World War and was an achievement of British military engineering. It matched the Quonset hut, invented in 1941 to fulfil the needs of the US Navy for a light, portable building that could be assembled quickly. The Quonset hut had been imported to Korea in August 1953. However, it was the Romney hut that the sappers preferred to use at the Castle Inn.

On 23 March 1954, the Royal Engineer diary entry reported, 'we have been informed that civilians are being allowed back into the divisional area to set up a village and carry out farming. They are providing their own village persons for mine clearance. A course will be set up to instruct twenty-four civilians in the "art", they will start clearing 10th of April 1954.'

The 1st Commonwealth Division resettlement conditions for any villagers were very strict. The civilians had to promise not to enter the DMZ, which was clearly signposted, and to stay within their specified boundaries at all times. The villagers were to carry a security pass at all times and surrender it for inspection to field security or the military police. Theft of UN property was not tolerated. It was made clear that if any person was caught with UN property, they and their entire family would be evacuated to the rear. All villagers were to be home by sunset and not leave again until dawn.

The minefield clearance course and engineering tasks perhaps strengthened the bond between the sappers and the civilian population who had always been

Above: *This hut was to be used as a theatre. Rickety-looking scaffolding towers were moved by hand across the floor and climbed to install the plasterboard lining secured by hook bolts.*

Right: *A showbiz mural was painted on the plywood wall at the front of the stage to add to the atmosphere of the shows that visiting theatre and movie stars would put on to entertain the troops.*

present. It was a population the NKPA were expected to infiltrate and attack to disrupt the elections for the ROK National Assembly. These would take place on Thursday, 20 May 1954.

In April 1954, work parties from 3 RAR Assault Pioneer Platoon, Support Company commenced work on Lone Pine Patrol Camp. The camp was on flat ground between the forward lozenge feature and the River Imjin. Its aim

Frank titled this photograph, 'Two Generals visit the construction site of the Castle Inn with a Korean Officer. Right is Captain Sharp, RE of 3 Troop 55 Field Squadron.'

was to allow UN soldiers to practise and train in the 'art' of patrolling. On the south bank of the River Imjin, the Royal Engineers established a bridging camp called Upnor. The camp was intended to place a greater emphasis on unit and team building as opposed to individual training. On 20 April 1954, the Royal Engineer diary entry recorded that, '55 Field Squadron carried out reconnaissance of minefields and booby-trapped areas in the GLOSTER HILL area. Records in this area are inaccurate and we hope to establish more concrete info.'

During April 1954, 55 Field Squadron also continued building work at the Castle Inn.

The vehicle park at the Castle Inn was full of an assortment of transports. Parked between the trucks was a caterpillar-tracked Oxford Carrier manufactured by the British company Morris Ltd. This armoured personnel carrier was the workhorse of the Royal Engineers. Weighing in at more than six tons, these carriers had traversed the River Imjin, carrying vital supplies and delivering troops into or extracting them from battle.

The Oxford Carrier was 14-feet long, 7-feet wide and 5-feet high with a crew of three. Its Cadillac V8 petrol, 5671cc engine, gave it a maximum speed of 31 miles per hour.

The generals inspected the ongoing construction work.

The inspection included testing the quality of the drinks at the Officers' Club at the Castle Inn.

Satisfied that the work was progressing well, the generals climbed back into their individual jeeps with their drivers and returned to headquarters.

Frank operated his camera with one hand as he saluted the commander of the Royal Engineers, Colonel Arthur Morris DSO MC GM. He saluted back with a smile as he was driven off. A QL office truck was parked next to a spoof construction-company sign made by the sappers who were building the Castle Inn. The sign, 'Labour Contractors Hannay & Hanna', was in homage to Major Spencer Hannay, Commanding Officer of 55 Field Squadron, who had left for the UK on 22 April 1954 having completed his tour of duty.

From 26 to 30 April 1954, the Commonwealth Division Exercise Impetus took place. It involved training to advance and attack and was scheduled in addition to ongoing operations.

Frank said, 'At some stage I had finally earned the right to call a sergeant, "Sarge". I went on patrol and was asked to look out for the new lads. Entering a home was strictly out of bounds unless we were ordered to search it. I clipped one of the new blokes around the ear and dragged him out. I explained that entry into the room with the best view was strictly forbidden, even to family members, as this was the room of the Buddha and, therefore, the house temple. With the external wall removed on a hot day, the room looked like a bare wooden porch and the new bloke had blundered into it to look at the view. Through open hand gestures we made our apologies to the family and rejoined our mates.'

A jeep patrol passes by an overturned artillery gun.

A Royal Signals jeep patrol travelled on a road masked from enemy observation by thatched screens constructed by the Royal Engineers. Canvas screens were also hung over roads on wire laced between 20-feet-high poles to further block the line of sight and prevent attack from enemy artillery and snipers.

A jeep patrol entering a village. Here, Frank's acquired knowledge of Korean life from his rebellious wandering with his camera was to be of use.

Frank's patrol set up camp in a cluster of trees with their vehicles hidden under camouflage netting.

Frank and his comrades assembled on parade. In the top right of the photograph is a Sten gun with two magazines taped together, facing the opposite way to each other. This would allow for a quick reload by pulling out the magazines from the gun, turning them round and plugging the full clip into the gun to continue firing. Frank said, 'I tried this myself when I was armed with a Sten gun for a night patrol. The tail-end Charlie of the patrol, who was a corporal, angrily came up and took the gun off me. As I'd been walking, I'd been dropping the bullets out of the spare magazine, leaving a trail for him to follow. After that, I stuck to a .303 rifle.'

Surrounded by their tents and vehicles, and hidden by camouflage netting, a meal is eaten, with one sapper keeping his bipod-mounted Bren gun close by. This was in case they suddenly found themselves in hostile contact with the NKPA guerrillas who were still active in South Korea.

During Exercise Impetus, a Centurion tank weighing in at 58 tons was too heavy for most bridges. The sappers' solution was to use the Class 60 raft fitted with an outboard motor. The class system defined the maximum weight that could be carried on a bridge or a raft.

The tank was boated along and across the river to where it was needed on the frontline. In a counter offensive, tanks could cross the river by the rafts in support of infantry equipped with assault boats, to surprise and outflank the enemy.

Peace talks resumed as part of a conference held with the communist nations, in Geneva on 26 April 1954. The Neutral Nations Supervisory Commission (NNSC) had previously been established to stop the deployment of additional military forces and weapons to Korea. The north cited the NNSC inspection reports from August 1953 to April 1954 as evidence of an increase of American weapons and personnel in the South. At the conference, it was proposed by America and South Korea that Chinese forces withdraw from North Korea and elections be held using the southern system. It was proposed that the United Nations forces stay on as an international police force. North Korea's counter proposal suggested the withdrawal of all forces as per the armistice agreement of 1953. They also proposed elections be held across all of Korea observed by the NNSC. The Korean component of the Geneva conference between the United Nations and Soviet Union failed to reach any agreement. The diplomats continued to discuss the Soviet-backed communist war against French colonial rule in Indochina. Indochina was dissolved into four separate nations: Cambodia, Laos, Soviet-sponsored Democratic Republic of Vietnam (North) and American-backed State of Vietnam (South). The Korean War was officially over to the politicians. Frank was adamant from what he had seen and heard that hostilities were continuing due to the activity of NKPA guerrillas. Both sides of the DMZ were ready to resume fighting on a large scale should the armistice end abruptly. The divisional front had been unusually quiet up to 30 April 1954, whereas previously observed activity in the DMZ had involved enemy sappers digging trenches and repairing bunkers to fortify their frontline. The number of sightings of 'civilians' supposedly collecting wood and carrying out farming had dropped.

On 1 May 1954, 55 Field Squadron and their attached Korean Service Corps labourers completed construction of the Castle Inn.

The Castle Inn   171

Having filled the fire buckets at the Castle Inn with sand, the sapper took them to the standing point.

The Castle Inn on the morning of its opening.

Major General Horatius Murray (centre) officially opened the Castle Inn.

General Murray was a Second World War veteran who had been wounded in the African desert campaign. He had subsequently fought in the Normandy and Italian campaigns. He had become the General in Overall Command (GOC) of the 1st Commonwealth Division on 12 October 1953.

Major General Murray has a private word with Captain Sharp, whose tour of duty was up. He was sent home on 5 May 1954. He had been 'Taken on Strength' with the 28 Field Regiment Royal Engineers on 29 April 1953.

The Castle Inn 173

The regimental band played at the tea party for the opening of the Castle Inn.

Fresh-faced, slightly bewildered and 'somewhat cheeky' younger replacements quickly down their drinks.

Veteran sappers enjoy a cup of tea and a slice of cake.

While touring the Castle Inn, the Romney hut housing the theatre, with its stage, mural and timbered floor that allowed seating to be raked during a show, was also inspected.

The friendly members of the Women's Voluntary Service lived and worked at the Castle Inn. They cooked a portion of chips that was served with a pint, for a soldier to enjoy as close to the crowded fireplace as he could get. It was a welcome break for those who had spent months on the frontline and for the truck drivers who brought supplies. It was courteous to return the cutlery, rather than take it with you, as it was costly to replace.

The WVS was admired for their courage under fire. Previously during the war, they had staffed NAAFI inns and fragile mobile kitchens just behind the frontline. The WVS women were undeterred by the shells exploding around them as they served up teas and a hot snack to the exhausted, battle-weary soldiers.

The Castle Inn was well stocked with a library of the latest magazines and newspapers, plus books donated by charitable groups in Britain.

In whatever camp you were in, the higher ranks received the newspapers first. The officers obtained their newspapers straight off the plane from London, but they were still the previous day's editions by the time they got them. Frank said, 'By the time they were passed to the lower ranks, the papers were several days old and the crossword the corporal had been looking forward to was often already filled in.'

The vehicle park was always crowded with sappers and soldiers coming or going to various camps or the frontline.

The war continued with constant operations to counter NKPA incursion as well as training exercises to prepare sappers and the infantry regiments they supported to repulse an invasion should it occur. For something to eat, Frank and his fellow sappers gathered around a table under camouflage netting. Here, they opened tinned food and sawed through bread that was as solid as a brick.

On 3 May 1954, an intelligence summary on enemy activity reported that 'a suspected violation of the DMZ occurred when 6 men with a suspected 82mm mortar were seen'. An 82mm mortar was able to launch twenty-five bombs per minute, capable of causing carnage in a crowded area such as the Castle Inn or a polling station on election day.

On 18 May 1954, standing orders were received that on 20 May – the day of elections to the ROK national assembly – polling stations were out of bounds to Commonwealth soldiers. The orders were explicit – no photographs were to be taken in these areas, so it could not be misconstrued that the elections were being influenced or interfered with.

From the middle of May 1954 until the month's end, 12 and 55 Field Squadrons provided valuable training to the Royal Australian Regiments in the use of M2 assault boats. This took place at Upnor camp on the bank of the Imjin, west of Teal Bridge. In a repeat of Exercise Impetus, 12 Field Squadron took part in the Australian exercise named Bondi. The sappers supplied the boats and rigged safety lines for the river crossing. They kept one assault boat back to use as a lifeboat, and rafts ferried support vehicles across the river.

The aim of Exercise Bondi was for the Australians to be able to cross a water obstacle and attack. The narrative of the exercise was that the communists had launched a surprise invasion to prevent the redeployment of UN forces from South Korea to the war in Indochina (South Vietnam). As the exercise continued on 1 June 1954, the sappers supervised 3 RAR's anti-tank platoon in laying a minefield using empty beer cans as dummy mines.

In June 1954, 12 Field and 55 Field Squadron officers attended the commando-style patrol training courses at the 3 RAR-established Lone Pine Patrol Camp. Daytime lectures included detecting and moving through minefields and across the obstacle-strewn, booby-trapped and fortified frontline at night. What they had learned, as well as taught from their own personal experiences, was then tested on a live night patrol. On 30 June 1954, at 23:59 hours, a Commonwealth patrol, dressed as commandos, with faces camouflaged, encountered a group of 'mysterious' Koreans at Yulp-P-Pri, in breach of the curfew. However, the patrol had been spotted and the Koreans withdrew before who they were and what they were up to could be established.

Chapter 16

Homeward Bound

Frank's service record revealed that on 17 July 1954, under Order 168, he was 'Struck of Strength' from the regimental list. Frank's National Service had until this point been one year and thirty-three days long. He was being sent home.

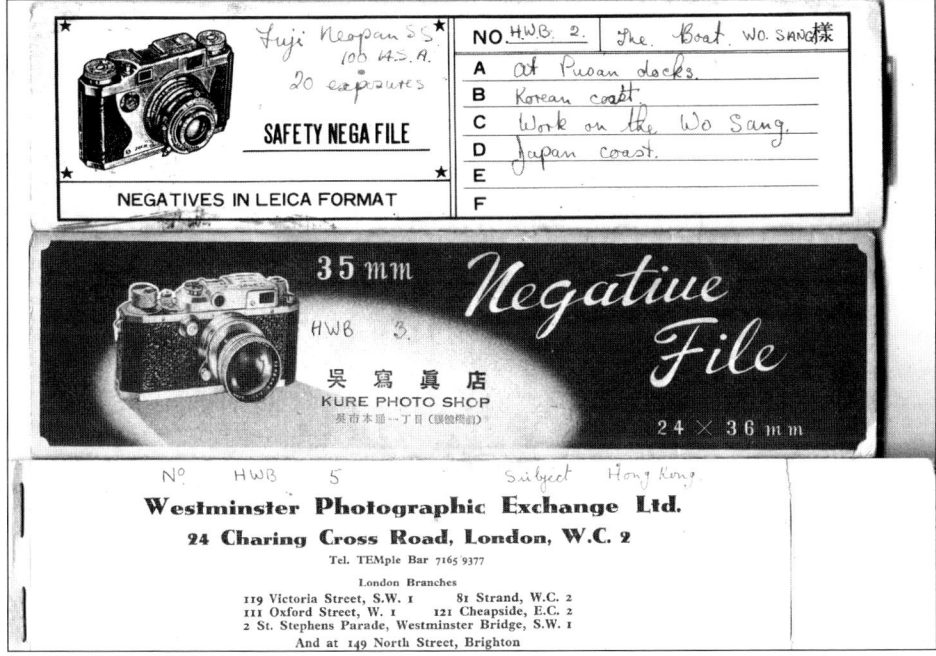

Frank marked 'HWB', which stood for homeward bound, on six negative albums. HWB 1, 2 and 3 were from a camera shop in Kure, Japan, and albums 4, 5 and 6 were from the 'Westminster Photographic Exchange Ltd'. The handwritten notes on the album fronts in pen gave the locations where the photographs were taken. Frank hadn't been able to use his cameras much on his outward journey to Korea due to the intense training he had experienced. He was determined to photograph his voyage home.

Being keen on trains, Frank was fascinated by this General Motors Electro-Motive Division, 100-ton SW8 diesel switcher locomotive No. 2031. It was painted black with white numbering and was 44-feet long, 9-feet wide and 14 feet in height. It ran on a standard 4-feet gauge track and had been shipped to Korea and operated throughout the war by the US Army 712th Transportation Railway Operating Battalion. This was a unit of volunteer train engineers called up from the Reading (Railroad) Company and the Central Railroad of New Jersey. They were just one of the battalions that had taken over the running of the Korean National Railway to ensure the troops and supplies reached where they needed to be.

On the train to Pusan, the troops were jam-packed into poky wooden carriages. They had to bed down on bunks as hard as church pews, with their tin helmets for pillows. The lance corporal in charge of Frank's section played chess to pass the time on the two-day journey south.

In the train, the carriages had no glass in their windows. As it snaked around a curve at a crossing, a dozen begging orphans in rags rushed along the road to the railway line. The children ran beside the train shouting for food, and some had rocks in their hand ready to pelt the train if they didn't get anything. It was a hard choice whether to let the orphans go hungry and stone the train or throw food to them. Frank said, 'If you threw out a food ration, they were going to fight over it with the big bullies winning. It seemed at every crossing and provincial station in the middle of nowhere, there were hungry children. We were sent to Korea to help and now we were going home, but the job didn't feel done. It was heartbreaking. Even the toughest among us choked up.'

The train ran between the paddy fields and farmland that surrounded small, thatched hamlets. It passed through a rain-washed freight yard with box carriages in sidings. The railway line ran adjacent to the River Han, with its boats that had the appearance of being made of matchsticks. 'Mud larks' (children) foraged for food along its banks.

The SS *Wo Sang 2* was originally named the *Hai Chen* and was one of many ships built by the London and Glasgow Engineering and Iron Shipbuilding Company. The vessel had been constructed in Yard 651 of the Barclay, Curle & Co Ltd shipyard in Glasgow in October 1934. The China Merchants Steam Navigation Co., Shanghai, China, had purchased the ship. In 1938, it had been sold to the Indo-China Steam Navigation Company Limited and renamed the *Wo Sang 2*. The company had been established in 1873 and was a subsidiary of Hong Kong-based Jardine, Matheson & Co., one of the largest trading companies in the Far East. The funnels of the ships were painted red with black tops. The *Wo Sang 2* was 328-feet long, 46-feet wide and able to carry 3000 tons. It had been chartered by the Ministry of War Transport in 1951, along with its sister ship the SS *E-Sang*. Both vessels ferried troops and cargo between Pusan, Korea and Kure in Japan.

As the ship sailed, Frank promised himself he would return to Korea one day. He never did. During the voyage, the menu for the officers and civilian passengers

After an overnight stay in the transit camp at Pusan, the homeward-bound troops went to the docks to board the SS Wo Sang 2. *It would be taking them to Japan.*

Boarding at Pusan Docks, the 400 soldiers had two kit bags each, with their serial number, surname and destination stencilled in paint on them. The soldier with the kit bag '22715410 Henstock KOREA TO UK' should have been the last in the line, but Frank stopped to take pictures. He was chased on board by a Port Squadron sapper shouting, 'Hurry up! Don't you want to go home?'

The ship is casting off with the departing troops on board. Pallets of stacked wooden crates marked 'NAAFI/EFI', which the ship had delivered, awaited distribution to the troops still remaining in Korea.

dining on the SS *Wo Sang 2* advertised a luncheon of Russian borscht, entrées of lobster mayonnaise, mutton curry and rice. On the menu, under the heading of cold meat, was pig's head brawn or roast prime of beef served with boiled potatoes, mixed vegetables or tomato and cucumber salad. For the 'sweet', it was a choice of stewed mixed fruit, cheese crackers, bread or toast served with tea or coffee.

The ship's crew worked on deck, while the soldiers collected tea or coffee in their mugs, to accompany their basic army rations eaten from their mess tins.

The ship was overcrowded. The 400 soldiers escaped the cramped, stinking conditions below by taking walks on deck to enjoy the fresh sea air.

The Wo Sang 2 *docked at Kure, Japan. The troops disembarked and boarded the American GMC trucks to be driven to the Joint Reinforcement Base Depot (JRBD). The British Commonwealth (BRITCOM) Engineer Regiment staffed it. They managed postings to the frontline, the Rest and Recuperation leave and the shipping home of the soldiers.*

Homeward Bound 185

The rooms of the barracks were warm, dry and well furnished. Frank said, 'It was luxury. Many blokes wrote a letter home.'

The hills of Kure City.

Inside the green cover of the 'Kure Photo Shop' album, Frank has written in pencil, 'Japan Kure, a walk from J.R.B.D. near Hiro.'

The hills of Kure were cut into agricultural pyramids for farming. When it rained, the water would flood each step, and be channelled around the housing in spectacular waterfalls to pool into the lake below. Sandwiched between these hills and its coastal port on the Inland Sea was the city of Kure. Frank said, 'It was an amazing sight. I fell in love with the place.'

Frank wandered city streets, where crowds passed the bars and restaurants full of servicemen from different nations. The department stores sold western fashions. At night, neon signs lit up the street in this photograph.

Next to the 'Tokyo Silk Co' (right of photograph) was the 'Originality' gift shop.

Frank said, 'The gift shop was where the blokes heading home found a present – usually a ladies' hand fan for a mother, wife, fiancée or sister. These were the only words in English the shopkeeper knew, and she seemed to know what pattern on the fan would be appropriate. I didn't speak Japanese and when I asked to take a picture, it caused a misunderstanding in which she was offended, thinking I was asking her out. This was soon cleared up by one of the lads who spoke Japanese.'

At Kure docks, Frank was about to board a troopship when he spotted the 149-feet-long US Army Large Tug-230. This steel tug had been built in 1943, to US Army design 254, at the Marietta Manufacturing Co., Point Pleasant, West Virginia. Launched in 1943, the tug had been put into service with the US Army Transportation Corps in February 1944. There was an old American saying, 'I joined the army, and they sent me to sea.'

On board the troopship heading to Hong Kong, Frank played a friendly game of chess, which attracted a crowd of spectators. Frank and the lance corporal had already established a reputation for being very good players.

During Frank's stay in Hong Kong, he took the tram up Mount Austin. It was also locally and more popularly known as Victoria Peak. The mountain was 1811-feet high and offered a panoramic view of Hong Kong.

Homeward Bound 189

Above: *Hong Kong in 1954.*

Right: *Frank toured Hong Kong and in this busy street of tailors' stores was the Cathay Arts Company. The Shanghai merchant Hoi Yu-lei had founded it in 1949. From 1950, Cathay Arts had met the increasing demand for camphor-wood chests and hand-carved wooden furniture, despite a US trade embargo. It was in its showroom that 'diplomats' from communist China happened upon British and American soldiers. As they all picked out furniture together, it was revealed that the 'diplomats' were in fact Chinese officers who had been directly opposite the British and Americans on the frontline in Korea. They now shared a common interest of buying the furniture and arranging it to be shipped home to their parents.*

190   The Royal Engineers in Korea: The Photographic Memoir of Frank Merritt

The building work on this street interested Frank more than seeing the films showing at the Alhambra Cinema opposite. The policeman (top left of photograph) stood beside a film poster for The Youth of Chopin *that was being screened. This was a 1952 Polish film written and directed by Aleksander Ford. The main feature being screened was* Dial M for Murder.

Frank and his comrades were to travel to Singapore on this troopship. The sampans alongside the ship formed a busy water market, trading with the soldiers who were already onboard.

Homeward Bound 191

The sampan was crammed with bread, pastries, fruit and vegetables, etc. There were bottles of fruit juice, soft drinks and beers. Frank remembered that everything had been 'low priced and good quality'.

On the troopship heading to Singapore, Frank met some Gurkhas. These Nepalese soldiers have served in the British Army for generations.

Sampan traders had plenty of customers as the troops remembered how bad the food had been on the ship that had taken them from Britain. They stocked up on what they considered luxuries, to enjoy on the first leg of the journey home. The traders hoisted the sold goods in baskets on poles to their customers. A brief ripple of surf was created by the fin of a shark as its shadowy outline circled between competing sampans. The shark lingered for a meal if a rare spillage occurred as the basket was lifted. Greater care was taken with the return of the basket, so as not to drop the money into the water, as the shark would apparently eat that too.

At the end of 1948, the Gurkha sapper squadrons had been created from the re-enlisted riflemen of the Gurkha regiments of the disbanded (British) Indian Army. In 1950, 67 and 68 Gurkha Field Squadrons Royal Engineers had been posted to Hong Kong to replace the British sapper units sent to Korea. In 1954, the Gurkhas were being deployed to combat the Chinese-backed communist terrorists of the Malayan Races Liberation Army.

An officer tried to organize a boxing match during the voyage. A regimental champion told the officer, 'I wouldn't last five minutes against a Gurkha, sir.'

Frank said, 'When I saw them on board I checked my boots, remembering what the Second World War veteran at Hara Mara had said about my boots being laced incorrectly. He had told me that when you move through the jungle, that's what the Gurkhas noticed first. If your boots were laced correctly, you were a friend and they'll let you by. Laced wrongly and you were the enemy. Then they'd ambush you and attack you with their kukris before you knew they were there.'

Frank thought the Gurkhas were, 'Good blokes – very friendly. They liked the ice cream the ship had been well-stocked with.'

Homeward Bound 193

At Singapore, art deco offices and apartment buildings sat beside dilapidated housing blocks with ground-floor shops and factories. They overlooked a crowded waterfront of working sampans and junks that doubled as homes.

Above the polluted surf that licked against the dockside, this dental patient sat cross-legged upon the quay, with head back and mouth open. The dentist worked with pliers pulling the tooth.

Above: *In a waterfront park, the snake charmer offered to entertain passing tourists. When the charmer removed the basket lid and played his bulbous flute (known as a pungi), the snake responded. As snakes can sense vibrations but cannot actually hear music, the pungi was crafted to appear as a predator to the snake. When the charmer played it, he moved from side to side and the snake rose on its tail from the basket, mirroring his movements, ready to defend itself. Snake charming was a cruel trade in which a captured snake was defanged, so a charmer could not be bitten. Several species of snakes became endangered because of it. It was the entertainers though, earning a few meagre coins, that became extinct in the 1950s and not the snakes.*

Opposite above left: *Rickshaw pullers waited in the Tanjong Pagar Road for customers newly arrived in Singapore. It was home to the families of the city's dockworkers and housed the 'Institute for Seamen' hostel. The rickshaw pullers were the fittest among the poorest residents, working long hours in all weathers for low pay. Being hit by a car was an occupational hazard.*

Opposite above right: *The city streets rang with the warning bells of the bicycle taxis whizzing through gridlocked traffic.*

Opposite below: *A busy street in Singapore.*

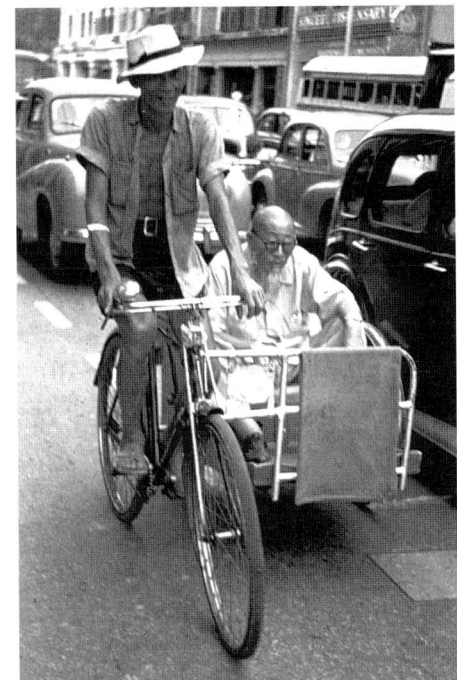

An aspiring entrepreneurial spirit of 'can do' and a 'must do' attitude ran through families in Singapore. It encouraged an abundance of street food stalls. Each stall was unique, offering European, Asian or Oriental food, or a meal that was a blend of all three cuisines. The culinary delights of pancakes, pasties and stews were prepared to family recipes, ensuring a dozen variations of the food available. This shut the American fast-food franchise industry out of Singapore as each small family business had a loyal customer base of residents. The 1000 hungry soldiers who came off a troopship added to this footfall. Soldiers took the opportunity to stock up for the start of the next leg of their journey home.

When the ship arrived at the busy international port of Colombo on the island of Ceylon (now Sri Lanka) in the Indian Ocean, Frank discovered it was very much like Singapore. Only a strip of Frank's photographs from Ceylon survives. The cow and wagon made its way through traffic on its delivery run.

Right: *As the troop ship sailed across the Arabian Sea, fishing rods replaced rifles, whereas on the outward voyage to Korea, the sea had been used as a firing range.*

Below: *To Frank, the Suez Canal was an incredible feat of engineering. Sun-bleached, weather-holed sails of raft-like Arab dhows caught the warm wind as they glided through the water to deliver cargo. The outline of the ship ahead and ships coming from the opposite direction made for a busy horizon.*

As the troop ship arrived at Port Said in Egypt, a crowded boat of traders pulled alongside. Pairs of shoes on top of their boxes and other goods were on display. When a price was agreed with a passenger on board, the item was bagged and winched up via the line that had been thrown to the customer. Frank said, 'They were known as bum boats, as they often sold shoddy goods and tourist tat. You paid up front for a pair of shoes and as soon as you put them on, the soles came off, with your feet going right through. The other bits and bobs they sold also fell apart as soon as you touched them, so they were slung back at the cheats in the boat. It was once caught, twice shy, as we'd traded with them on the journey out. We were wise to them when going home.'

The Suez Canal is a strategically important shipping lane connecting Europe to the Middle East, India and the Far East. The canal separated Egypt from the Sinai Peninsula, and the British presence in the region allowed for Britain to monopolize international trade. Following the 1948–49 Arab-Israeli war, tension between the three countries had increased, with Egyptian nationalists disappointed with the timetable set for the British withdrawal from Egypt. Looking across the Sinai, all Frank saw was a flat desert populated by a line of telegraph poles. There was no sign of the dug-in Egyptian or British troops locked in a cold war.

Frank arrived back in England on his birthday of 30 August 1954. He was aged 22. His service record states that he then reported to the Royal Engineer depot at Barton Stacey. An order was raised (No. 171) to post him to B Squadron. Order 172 struck him from the list on 2 September 1954, and on 3 September, his service record was stamped 'Terminal Leave Granted'.

Frank said, 'I'd written to Dad to say I was coming home. When I got out of the train at London, I stood on the platform waiting for my connection and lit a roll-up. As the steam from the locomotive cleared, I saw Dad standing there. He'd come up to meet me. He disapproved of smoking, but he didn't say a word, just wiped a tear from his eye. That's when I realized I was almost home.'

On 26 September 1954, Frank was discharged, and his service record was stamped 'Military Conduct Very Good'. On 27 September, he reported to begin part-time National Service, joining the 211 (Thames and Medway) Field Squadron Royal Engineers. The 211 were part of the 119 Field Engineers Regiment Territorial Army Reserve and their HQ was actually in Brighton, Sussex. The 211 made regular trips to the coastal town for training. In the 1950s, Brighton had a rather seedy reputation, and Frank was a role model to his comrades and, perhaps, a reminder to any 'flash Harry' spivs of their own shortcomings. Oddly, despite having wandered alone and unarmed through Korean villages either side of the frontline, Frank didn't dare walk down certain Brighton streets. He did though become a regular customer of the town's camera shops.

Frank at home.

The training recommendation and the job he was offered with the 211 was general duties clerk but, worried about his dyslexia, he turned it down. He also refused promotion. Frank need not have worried. He had better handwriting than many, as evidenced by his service record, which is marked in some places with an officer's unreadable scribble.

'Student' was listed in the civilian occupation box on Frank's service record while serving with 211. The Royal Engineers trained the sappers for future employment in a trade industry after their two years of National Service was completed and they were demobbed.

Having been discharged on 3 March 1958 and placed on the reserve list, Frank bought himself a motorcycle to tour England, Wales and Scotland. He was determined to visit every part of the country he had dutifully served, photographing the people and places from the smallest village to the largest city. Over the decades, Frank amassed thousands of photographs across a wide range of subjects. He repeatedly won trophies at his camera club and was asked to put on an exhibition of his prints and slides at his local town hall. The Royal Mail invited him to give a slide lecture on the history of post boxes. However, Frank didn't show his Korean archive to anyone.

Above left: *Frank trained to be a silversmith. His tutor was Sidney James Sparrow, whose registered hallmark was S.J.S. Sparrow taught at the London Central School of Arts and Crafts. Frank forged a communion chalice and plate that he later donated to his family church of St Paulinus, Crayford, to use in services.*

Above right: *Frank forged what became known as the Merritt Rose Bowl. He had developed his own unique crimping technique that other silversmiths couldn't replicate. This made the bowl a one of a kind. Frank donated it to Goldsmiths Hall silver collection.*

In the 1970s, Frank and I visited the Royal Engineers Museum in Gillingham, Kent. This was before it was separated from the Royal Engineer barracks and visitors walked around the edge of the parade ground. Sappers were square-bashing before a sergeant who had a swagger stick tucked into his armpit. He noticed my middle-aged father, as always dressed in a suit and tie, as he passed by with me, his then infant son. The sergeant called the men to a halt and then made the sappers parade in perfect symmetry. He turned on his heels to reveal a chest full of medal ribbons including those for the Korean War. The parade saluted Frank.

In the twenty-first century, on another trip to the museum, a now elderly Frank met with Korean delegates. As he talked with them, one recognized Frank and remembered that as a boy he had been photographed by him, as he wandered through his village. The delegate had later discovered that Frank's presence that day had deterred an NKPA guerrilla raid. The bandits had not realized Frank was there on his own. The delegate said, 'Thank you. If it wasn't for you, I and my family would not be alive today.'

In 2010, at the age of 78, Frank became terminally ill. In his sleep, his hands held an imaginary 35mm camera, his finger pressing down on the shutter. In his sleep, he escaped the hospital bed, reliving his exploration of Korea. In his final days, he talked of his time there, remembering how once, after one of his unofficial excursions, his sergeant had asked, 'Where've you been, Frank?'

'North Korea,' Frank had replied, to the other man's shock. The sergeant had known this was the truth as Frank wasn't known for joking around. On one of his final days, lying in hospital, Frank told me, 'I'm going to see what's on the other side of the hill before the light fades.'

Today, North and South Korea are still considered officially at war and the DMZ is the most heavily fortified border in the world and the scene of sporadic fighting. Infiltration tunnels to breach it were discovered in the 1970s and intelligence reports stated they were large enough for an entire NKPA regiment to pass through. Over the years, North Koreans have also landed on the heavily patrolled but vulnerable coastline. Peace talks have continued, and my father's last wish was that the Korean people as a whole could eventually find a way to a peaceful co-existence. Frank Merritt died on 12 November 2010. He was 78.

Acknowledgements

Thank you to

Judy Upton

James Wright and Yvonne Allen, administrative officers at the Army Personnel Centre, Historical Disclosures

Rebecca Blackburn and the staff at the Royal Engineers Museum, Gillingham

All the team at Pen & Sword Books

Bibliography and Sources

Books

A Barren Place, Adrian Walker, Pen and Sword Books
A Conscript in Korea, Neville Williams, Pen and Sword Books
From the Imjin to The Hook, James Jacobs, Pen and Sword Books
Fight, Dig and Live, George Cooper, Pen and Sword Books
Eyewitness Korea, James Goulty, Pen and Sword Books
Follow The Sapper, Gerald Napier, Institution of Royal Engineers
History of the Corps of Royal Engineers, Volume X, Institution of Royal Engineers
The Encyclopedia of the Korean War, Spencer C Tucker, ABC-CLIO
Korea: The Commonwealth at War, Tim Carew, Cassell
The British Army Today and Tomorrow, Colonel H.C.B. Rogers, Ian Allen Ltd
Nothing To Envy: Real Lives in Korea, Barbara Deniwick, Granta Publications
One Road to the Imjin, D.E. Whatmore, Dew Line Publications
The Korean War, Max Hastings, Pan Books
Edge of the Sword, Captain Anthony Farrar-Hockley, Frederick Muller Ltd
Korea: The Unknown War, John Halliday and Bruce Cumins, Viking
At War in Korea, George Forty, Arms and Armour
The Korean War: The West Confronts Communism 1950–1953, Michael Hickey, John Murray Ltd
Culture and Customs of Korea, Donald N Clark, Greenworld Publishing
The Corps of Engineers: Troops and Equipment, Blanche D. Coil, Jean E. Keith and Herbert H. Rosenthal, Center of Military History, United States Army
Bridging The Imjin: Construction of Libby and Teal Bridges During the Korean War, William R. Farquhar, Jr and Henry A. Jeffers, Jr, Office of History, United States Army Corps of Engineers
The Earthmover Encyclopedia, Keith Haddock, Motorbooks International
Buddhist Art And Architecture, Robert E. Fisher, Thames and Hudson World of Art
Abode Photoshop 6.0 for Photographers, Martin Evening, Focal Press
The Complete Guide to Digital Photography, Michael Freeman, Ilex Press

Military manuals, documents, museums, newspapers and websites

War Office: British Commonwealth Division of United Nations Force War Diaries, Korean War (WO 281)
Royal Engineers Korean War Diaries, Royal Engineers Museum, Gillingham
The Royal Engineers Journal, Royal Engineers Museum, Gillingham
The Corps of Royal Engineers pamphlet, 1950
Royal Engineers Museum
Imperial War Museum
National Army Museum
Army Flying Museum
Korean Stone Art Museum
Crypto Museum (cryptomuseum.com)
Portsmouth Evening News, April 1953
Korean Times (www.koreatimes.co.kr)
Evening Advocate, Friday, 24 April 1953
Small Farmer's Journal (www.smallfarmersjournal.com)
Canal Zoners (canalzoners.co.uk)
Troopship (Amenities), Hansard, HC Deb., Vol 493, cols 796-7 (13 November 1951)
Caledonian Maritime Research Trust
On Walkabout Travel and Hiking Network (https://on-walkabout.net)
New World Encyclopedia (www.newworldencyclopedia.org)
United States Army and Air Force Locomotives (www.military.railfan.net)
Krigsseilerregisteret (www.krigsseilerregisteret.no)
NavSource Naval History (www.navsource.org/archives/armyidx.htm)
The Industrial History of Hong Kong Group (https://industrialhistoryhk.org)
Graces Guide to British Industrial History (https://gracesguide.co.uk)